CHINA
AND ITS
CUISINE

MALLARD
PRESS

*Happy Anniversary
to two wonderful people

Love
Maria & Larry
1990*

Recipes Selected and Edited by Jane Adams
Designed by Philip Clucas
Food Photography by Peter Barry and
    Neil Sutherland
Illustrations of China reproduced courtesy of
China Pictorial Publications, Beijing

MALLARD PRESS

An imprint of BDD Promotional Book Company, Inc.,
666 Fifth Avenue, New York, N.Y. 10103.
Mallard Press and its accompanying design and logo
are trademarks of BDD Promotional Book Company, Inc.

CLB 2369
Copyright © 1990 Colour Library Books Ltd.,
Godalming, Surrey, England.
Text filmsetting by Words and Spaces, Hampshire England.
First published in the United States of America
in 1990 by the Mallard Press.
Printed and bound in Hong Kong.
All rights reserved
ISBN 0 792 45225 9

CHINA
AND ITS
CUISINE

CONTENTS

Title: Pork and Shrimp Chow Mein. Previous pages: competitors prepare for the Dragon Boat Race in Foshan, Kwangtung province (main picture). Sweet-Sour Fish (inset). These pages: a restored section of the Great Wall of China.

INTRODUCTION

The popularity of Chinese cuisine has blossomed since the first Chinese emigrants exported their enticing and exotic flavors to the four corners of the globe. Today, Chinese cuisine has acquired a special place in the hearts of Americans. As well as being delicious, Chinese cuisine is regarded as being extremely healthful. The great variety and goodness of the ingredients in Chinese cookery, and its cooking methods, also ensure that it is one of the most nutritious cuisines in the world.

As the popularity of the dishes has grown, so has an interest in their origins. This book gives the cook an insight into the regional variations within China, introducing some traditional local dishes, but also including some which enjoy widespread popularity.

The regions of China vary greatly both in the availability of produce and in the type of flavor which the locals endorse. Northern tastes are much more conservative than those of the south, due partly to the harsh climate and the limited variety of crops. The neighboring Mongols have also left a lasting influence on the northern cuisine, instilling a love of lamb which is still much in evidence today. The capital of China is situated in the north and is home to one of the nation's most popular dishes, Peking Duck. Although the recipe seems rather expensive and complicated to make, the cook's efforts are well rewarded with a magnificent dish which will impress the most critical gourmet.

As might be expected, the eastern coastal region mixes the best of the northern and southern cuisines. This fertile, wet region produces a plentiful and varied harvest, the favorite ingredient being seafood. Local chefs utilize this abundant wealth to create gastronomic delights which combine the imaginative arts of the south with the solid simplicity of northern cooking.

The cuisine of western China is also currently enjoying great popularity. Szechuan is a mountainous region of western China where the climate is hot and humid and the people "down to earth." Crops tend to be grown in the plains which surround the capital of the region, Chengtu. Although the finite supply of fertile land means that the variety of crops is limited, the people of the region compensate for this by creating very pungent and highly spiced flavors. In complete contrast to the south, it is flavor and freshness rather than color and appearance that are the crucial factors.

Southern China, with its mild climate and great wealth of produce, is undoubtedly the most blessed region. The fertility of the land and the proximity of the sea provide an enormous variety of ingredients for the lavish and cosmopolitan dishes it is so famous for. Canton is the capital city of this area and is generally regarded as the culinary capital of China. Just as New York restaurants are regarded as sophisticated by out-of-towners, so it is with the Cantonese. Poultry, fish and an array of vegetables are very popular, and greater importance is attached to color and appearance than to strong flavor. Southerners prefer to utilize ingredients to provide taste rather than develop it with strong herbs or spices. Dim Sum was first introduced by the Cantonese and this popular array of appetizers is now loved by all those who adore Chinese food.

The first Chinese restaurant owners in America quickly discovered their clients favored very sweet or spicy flavors, and in true Chinese style they concocted dishes to please their guests. Although we think of dishes such as Chicken Chow Mein or Chicken Chop Suey as being quintessentially Chinese, they are not actually authentic Chinese recipes. They are nonetheless extremely tasty and continue to be a popular choice in restaurants.

China and its Cuisine offers a wealth of experiences as varied and exciting as the landscape and its people. Once you begin to explore the delights of cooking Chinese food you will be amazed at the ease of creating such tasty delights. Good luck on your culinary adventure!

Facing page: the Lijiang River flows slowly past strangely shaped needles of eroded limestone in northeast Kwangs Chuang.

SERVES: 4-6

Crab & Sweetcorn Soup

Creamy sweetcorn and succulent crabmeat combine to make a velvety
rich soup. Whisked egg whites add an interesting texture.

PREPARATION TIME: 10 minutes
COOKING TIME: 8-10 minutes

3½ cups chicken or fish stock
12oz cream style corn
4oz crabmeat
Salt and pepper
1 tsp light soy sauce

2 tbsps cornstarch
3 tbsps water or stock
2 egg whites, whisked
4 green onions, to garnish

Bring the stock to the boil in a large pan. Add the corn, crabmeat, seasoning and soy
sauce. Allow to simmer for 4-5 minutes.

Mix the cornstarch with the water or stock and add a spoonful of the hot soup.
Return the mixture to the soup and bring back to the boil. Cook until the soup
thickens.

Whisk the egg whites until soft peaks form. Stir into the hot soup just before
serving. Slice the onions thinly on the diagonal and scatter over the top to serve.

*Facing page: Mount Panshan in Tientsin is reputed to be the most
beautiful mountain east of the capital, Peking.*

SERVES: 6

Shark's Fin Soup

Shark's fin is added to this nutritious soup to give it texture.

PREPARATION TIME: 10 minutes, plus overnight soaking
COOKING TIME: 2 hours 10 minutes

½ cup shark's fin
3-4 slices fresh ginger root,
    shredded
8 Chinese dried mushrooms
5 cups chicken broth
1 tsp salt
1 tbsp dark soy sauce

1 cup crab meat
½lb cooked chicken meat,
    shredded
2 tbsps cornstarch blended in 5
    tbsps water
½ tsp sesame oil

Soak shark's fin overnight. Drain, simmer in 5 cups water with the shredded ginger root for 1½ hours. Drain. Simmer again in fresh water for 45 minutes. Remove and drain.

Soak mushrooms overnight. Drain. Remove stems, and quarter caps. Heat the broth in a ceramic pot. When boiling add the mushrooms and fin. Simmer for 15 minutes. Add the salt, soy sauce, and crab meat. Bring to a boil. Boil for 2-3 minutes. Add the shredded chicken, and cornstarch mixture. Bring to a boil. Stir for 3-4 minutes. Sprinkle with sesame oil and serve.

Facing Page: the Xiangtang Grottoes, Hopeh, possess this magnificent Buddhist statue among their many treasures.

SERVES: 6-8

Wonton Soup

Probably the best-known Chinese soup, this recipe uses ready-made
wonton wrappers for ease of preparation.

PREPARATION TIME: 25-30 minutes
COOKING TIME: 5-10 minutes

20-24 wonton wrappers
3oz finely ground chicken or pork
2 tbsps chopped Chinese parsley
3 green onions, finely chopped
1-inch piece fresh ginger, peeled
   and grated
1 egg, lightly beaten

5 cups chicken stock
1 tbsp dark soy sauce
Dash sesame oil
Salt and pepper
Chinese parsley or watercress, to
   garnish

Place all the wonton wrappers on a large, flat surface. Mix together the chicken or
pork, chopped parsley, green onions and ginger. Brush the edges of the wrappers lightly
with beaten egg. Place a small mound of mixture on one half of the wrappers and fold
the other half over the top to form a triangle. Press with the fingers to seal the edges
well.

   Bring the stock to the boil in a large saucepan. Add the filled wontons and simmer
5-10 minutes or until they float to the surface. Add remaining ingredients to the soup,
using only the leaves of the parsley or watercress as a garnish.

*Crescent Moon Spring, a small desert lake, lies at the start of a seemingly infinite stretch of the
Kansu Desert.*

SERVES: 4-6

Duck Carcass Soup

At the end of a Peking Duck dinner, it is customary to serve this soup which simply consists of the duck carcass, water and a few simple ingredients.

PREPARATION TIME: 10 minutes
COOKING TIME: 30 minutes

½ Chinese cabbage
2 cakes bean curd
2 tbsps soy sauce

1 tbsp vinegar
5 cups water

Cut the cabbage into 2-inch pieces. Cut the bean curd into ½-inch pieces. Place the duck carcass in a large pan with the cabbage, bean curd, soy sauce and vinegar. Add cold water to cover. Bring to a boil. Simmer for 30 minutes. Remove carcass and serve soup.

Jiuquan, meaning "Wine Spring," is the name given to a tranquil park in Kansu.

SERVES: 4-6

Hot & Sour Soup

A very warming soup, this is a favorite in winter in Peking. Add chili
sauce and vinegar to suit your taste.

PREPARATION TIME: 25 minutes
COOKING TIME: 7-8 minutes

2oz pork
3 dried Chinese mushrooms,
    soaked in boiling water for 5
    minutes and chopped
2oz peeled, uncooked shrimp
5 cups chicken stock
1oz bamboo shoots, sliced
3 green onions, shredded
Salt and pepper
1 tbsp sugar

1 tsp dark soy sauce
½ tsp light soy sauce
1-2 tsps chili sauce
1½ tbsps vinegar
Dash sesame seed oil and rice wine
    or sherry
1 egg, well beaten
2 tbsps water mixed with 1 tbsp
    cornstarch

Trim any fat from the pork and slice it into shreds about 2 inches long and less than
¼ thick. Soak the mushrooms in boiling water until softened. Place the pork in a large
pot with the shrimp and stock. Bring to the boil, then reduce the heat and simmer
gently for 4-5 minutes. Add all the remaining ingredients except for the egg and the
cornstarch and water mixture. Cook a further 1-2 minutes over a low heat.

    Remove the pan from the heat and add the egg gradually, stirring gently until it
forms threads in the soup. Mix a spoonful of the hot soup with the cornstarch and
water mixture and then add it to the soup, stirring constantly. Bring the soup back to
simmering point for 1 minute to thicken. Serve immediately.

Lhasa, the Tibetan capital, is located in the foothills of the Himalayas.

Crispy Wontons with Sauce

Wonton wrappers are readily available from most Chinese supermarkets.
Wrap small amounts of stuffing in the wrappers, press the edges together
well and deep-fry for 2-4 minutes until very crisp. Stuffings may consist of
almost any ingredient – ground pork with chopped shrimp is especially
delicious when topped with this sweet and sour sauce.

PREPARATION TIME: 15 minutes
COOKING TIME: 6-9 minutes

1 tbsp cornstarch	1 tbsp soy sauce
1 tbsp tomato paste	2 tbsps sugar
1 tbsp vinegar	1½ tbsps oil

Place all the sauce ingredients in a pan, and stir together over medium heat for 4-5
minutes.

*Batou Spring Park in Jinan, the capital of Shantung province,
contains fifteen natural springs.*

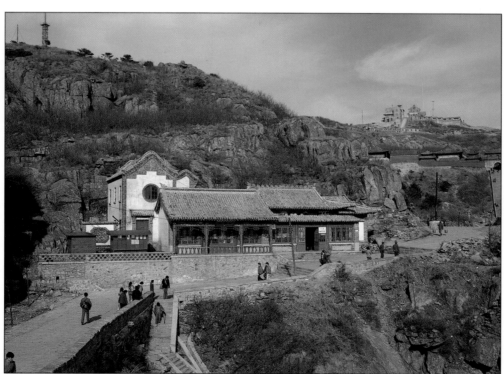

Heavenly Street on Mount Taishan - the mountain is one of China's holy mountains and, as a deity itself, is an object of pilgrimage.

SERVES: 4

Paotzu Steamed Buns with Pork, Cabbage and Mushrooms

These little buns might form part of a "Dim Sum" menu or serve as an appetizer to a Western meal.

PREPARATION TIME: 40 minutes, plus 2 hours rising time
COOKING TIME: 10 minutes

---

3 cups self-rising flour
1 cup warm water
1 tsp fresh yeast
1lb cabbage
6 black Chinese mushrooms,
   pre-soaked

1 tbsp chopped fresh ginger root
½lb ground pork
1 tbsp salt
1 tbsp soy sauce
1 tsp pepper
1 tsp sesame oil

Place the flour in a large bowl. Sprinkle the yeast on the warm water, stir and leave for 10 minutes, until frothy. Add the liquid to the flour, stir well. Leave in a warm place for 2 hours or until doubled in size.

Chop the cabbage, mushrooms and ginger. Add the pork, soy sauce, pepper and sesame oil. Mix well.

Knead the dough for a few minutes. Cut into 1½-inch pieces. Press a little of the pork mixture into each piece of dough. Shape into small round buns. Leave for 15-20 minutes. Place in a steamer and steam vigorously for 10 minutes. Serve immediately.

Facing page: the Hanging Monastery in the Heng Mountains of Shansi province is a truly remarkable feat of engineering dating back over 1,400 years.

SERVES: 4-6

Pork & Shrimp Chow Mein

Based on noodles, chow mein dishes use expensive ingredients in only small amounts and so make economical everyday meals.

PREPARATION TIME: 20 minutes
COOKING TIME: 12-16 minutes

8oz medium dried Chinese
   noodles
3 tbsps oil
8oz pork fillet, thinly sliced
1 carrot, peeled and shredded
1 small red pepper

3oz bean sprouts
2oz pea pods
1 tbsp rice wine or dry sherry
2 tbsps soy sauce
4oz peeled, cooked shrimp

Cook the noodles in plenty of boiling salted water for about 4-5 minutes. Rinse under hot water and drain thoroughly.

Heat a wok and add the oil. Stir-fry the pork 4-5 minutes or until almost cooked. Add the carrots to the wok and cook for 1-2 minutes. Core, seed and slice the red pepper and add the remaining vegetables, wine and soy sauce. Cook for about 2 minutes. Add the cooked, drained noodles and shrimp and toss over heat for 1-2 minutes. Serve immediately.

The entrance to the Mogao Caves near Dunhuang, Kansu, where hundreds of Buddhist cave temples are set in the sandstone cliff face.

MAKES: about 20 parcels

Rice Paper Shrimp Parcels

Try serving these appetizing parcels as a snack with pre-dinner drinks.

PREPARATION TIME: 15 minutes
COOKING TIME: 15 minutes

8oz shrimp, shelled and deveined
1 egg white
½ tsp cornstarch
1 tsp Chinese wine, or 2 tsps dry
   sherry
1 tsp sugar

1 tsp light soy sauce
6 green onions, sliced finely
Salt
Pepper
⅔ cup peanut oil
1 packet rice paper

Dry the prepared shrimp on paper towels. Mix the egg white, cornstarch, wine, sugar, soy sauce, green onions and seasoning together. Mix in the shrimp. Heat the peanut oil in a wok until hot. Wrap five or six shrimp in each piece of rice paper. Gently drop the rice paper parcels into the hot oil and deep-fry for about 5 minutes. Serve hot.

*Peking's beautiful Temple of Buddhist Virtue overlooks a lily pond
in the grounds of the Summer Palace.*

SERVES: 4

Crouton Studded "Pomegranate" Crispy Prawn Balls

The unusual appearance of these prawn balls makes them a useful
addition to the hors d'oeuvre table.

PREPARATION TIME: 30 minutes
COOKING TIME: 3 minutes per batch

---

4 slices white bread
½lb whitefish fillets
½lb shrimp (fresh or frozen)
2 tsps salt
Pepper to taste

2 egg whites
2 slices ginger root
2 tbsps cornstarch
Oil for deep-frying

Remove the crusts from the bread. Cut each slice into small crouton-sized cubes. Dry
in a hot oven until slightly browned. Spread out on a large tray. Chop the fish and
shelled shrimp very finely. Mix together with the salt, pepper, egg whites, finely
chopped ginger, and cornstarch. Blend well. Shape the mixture into 2-inch balls. Roll
these over the croutons to coat. Heat the oil in a deep-fat fryer. Add the crouton
studded prawn balls one by one. Turn with a perforated spoon until evenly browned,
about 2 minutes. Remove and drain. Return to the oil for a further 1 minute frying.
Drain well on paper towels. Serve with a good quality soy sauce, ketchup or chili sauce
as dips.

*Camel caravans were once a common sight at Yangguan Pass as
they travelled the old Silk Road.*

SERVES: 4

Sesame Prawn Toasts

A quickly-prepared snack that tastes wonderful anytime, so don't save it
just for Chinese meals.

PREPARATION TIME: 10 minutes
COOKING TIME: 5 minutes

½ cup pork fat
½ cup cooked shrimp
1 egg white
Salt and pepper to taste

1 tbsp cornstarch
2 slices white bread
6 tbsps sesame seeds
Oil for deep-frying

Finely chop the pork fat and shrimp. Blend together well with the egg white, salt,
pepper and cornstarch. Spread this paste thickly on the 2 slices of bread. Remove the
crusts. Sprinkle the paste thickly with sesame seeds pressing them on well. Heat the
oil. Lower one slice of bread at a time into the hot oil, spread side down, and fry for 2
minutes. Turn over and fry the other side for ½ minute. Repeat for the other slice of
bread. Cut each prawn toast in half, then into finger-sized strips. Serve hot.

*Above: delicious Crispy Seaweed and Sesame Shrimp Toasts are a
mouthwatering combination for a light meal or snack.*

SERVES: 4

Crispy Seaweed

Light and full of vitamins, this is definitely a dish for the health conscious.

PREPARATION TIME: 35 minutes
COOKING TIME: 5 minutes

2lbs greens
4 tbsps split almonds
Oil for deep-frying

½ tsp salt
1½ tsps sugar

With a very sharp knife, cut the greens into the finest shreds possible. Dry, by spreading them out on paper towels for ½ hour. Deep-fry, or shallow-fry the almonds until golden. Drain well. Heat the oil until it is about to smoke. Remove from the heat for ½ minute. Add all the shredded greens. Stir and return pan to the heat and fry for 2-3 minutes. Remove and drain well. Serve on a well heated platter, sprinkled evenly with salt, sugar, and the fried almonds.

Above: some of the 6,000 terracotta warriors found near the Xi'an tomb of Qin Shihuang, the first emperor to unify China.

SERVES: 8

Sesame Chicken Wings

This is an economical appetizer that is also good as a cocktail snack or as a
light meal with stir-fried vegetables.

PREPARATION TIME: 25 minutes
COOKING TIME: 13-14 minutes

12 chicken wings
1 tbsp salted black beans
1 tbsp water
1 tbsp oil
2 cloves garlic, crushed
2 slices fresh ginger, cut into fine
   shreds

3 tbsps soy sauce
1½ tbsps dry sherry or rice wine
Large pinch black pepper
1 tbsp sesame seeds
Green onions or Chinese parsley,
   to garnish (optional)

Cut off and discard the wing tips. Cut between the joint to separate each wing into
two pieces. Crush the beans and add the water. Leave to stand.

Heat the oil in a wok and add the garlic and ginger. Stir briefly and add the chicken
wings. Cook, stirring, until lightly browned, about 3 minutes. Add the soy sauce and
wine and cook, stirring, about 30 seconds longer. Add the soaked black beans and
pepper. Cover the wok tightly and allow to simmer for about 8-10 minutes. Uncover
and turn the heat to high. Continue cooking, stirring, until the liquid is almost
evaporated and the chicken wings are glazed with sauce. Remove from the heat and
sprinkle on the sesame seeds. Stir to coat completely and serve. Garnish with green
onions or Chinese parsley, if desired.

*The sheer size of Tiananmen Square, bordered by canals (above),
means that it has always been a central gathering place for the
people of Peking.*

MAKES: 12

Spring Rolls

A perennial favorite, spring rolls are delicious on their own or as part of a
selection of Chinese hors d'oeuvres.

PREPARATION TIME: 20-30 minutes
COOKING TIME: about 20 minutes

2 cups lean, raw pork or beef,
    finely shredded
1 cup small to medium, shelled
    shrimp (either uncooked or
    boiled)
4 green onions, finely chopped
1 tbsp oil
2 tsps fresh root ginger, peeled and
    shredded
1⅓ cups white cabbage, shredded

1-1¼ cups bean sprouts
1¼ tbsps soy sauce
Salt to taste
12 spring roll wrappers, each
    6 inches square (see recipe)
2 tbsps all-purpose flour, mixed
    with a little cold water to a
    smooth paste

Fry the shredded pork and the shrimp with the green onions in 1 tbsp oil for 2-3
minutes. Add the ginger, cabbage and bean sprouts, and stir-fry for 2-3 minutes. Add
the soy sauce, and season with a little salt if desired.

Remove from the heat and allow to cool. Lay out the spring roll wrappers on a clean
working surface, with one point of each wrapper facing you. Divide the filling mixture
into 12 equal portions and place one portion of filling just above the front point of
each wrapper. Fold in the opposite side points, so that they overlap slightly like an
envelope – secure the side points with a little flour and water paste. Starting with the
point facing you, roll each wrapper up around the filling, securing the remaining point
with a little flour and water paste. Repeat in exactly the same way with the remaining
spring roll wrappers. They will keep their shape better if you chill them for 1 hour
before cooking. Deep-fry over a medium heat until golden brown and crisp. Drain
thoroughly on absorbent paper and serve hot with a selection of dips or chili sauce.
The spring rolls can be frozen uncooked.

MAKES: 12 wrappers

Spring Roll Wrappers

PREPARATION TIME: 20 minutes, plus chilling time

1 cup strong plain flour
1 egg, beaten

A little cold water

Sift the flour into a bowl. Make a well in the center and add the beaten egg and a little
cold water. Mix to a soft yet firm dough, adding a little extra water if necessary. Knead
the dough until it is really pliable. (This helps to make the gluten work.) Chill,
covered, for 4 hours or overnight. Allow to come back to room temperature. Roll out
the dough on a well-floured surface to about ¼ inch thick. Cut into 12 equal pieces,
and then roll each piece very thinly to a 6-inch square.

*Facing page: Spring Rolls (center), Fried Meat Dumplings
(top), and Wontons with Pork and Shrimp Filling (bottom)
can be served with a chili sauce dip for extra piquancy.*

MAKES: 48 dumplings

Fried Meat Dumplings

Dumplings of many varieties are an important part of the Chinese "Dim Sum", an Oriental version of snacking!

PREPARATION TIME: 10 minutes
COOKING TIME: about 15 minutes

---

2 tbsps salad or olive oil
2 cups lean ground beef or lamb
2 green onions, chopped
2½ tbsps light soy sauce
½ tsp salt
1¾ tbsps rice wine or dry sherry

2 tsps cornstarch mixed with 2 tbsps water
Dumpling wrappers (see separate recipe)
2 tbsps all-purpose flour mixed to a paste with cold water
Oil for deep frying

Heat the 2 tbsps oil in a pan and fry the ground meat and onion for 2-3 minutes. Add the soy sauce, salt and wine. Cook gently for 2 minutes and then stir in the cornstarch and water mixture. Stir over the heat until the mixture thickens. Put the meat mixture into a dish and leave to cool. Divide into equal portions – about 48. Take a round dumpling wrapper and place a portion of filling in the center. Moisten the edges of the wrapper with a little flour and water paste, gather the edges up and over the filling and pinch together to seal. Shape neatly. Continue to make the remaining dumplings in the same way. Deep-fry the dumplings in moderately hot oil, cooking a few dumplings at a time, until they are golden brown. Drain thoroughly on paper towels. Serve with chili sauce dip.

Dramatic skies over Nanning, the subtropical capital city of Kwangs Chuang in southern China.

MAKES: 40-50 wrappers

Dumpling Wrappers

PREPARATION TIME: 50-60 minutes

2¼ cups all-purpose flour   ¾ cup cold water

Sift the flour into a bowl and add the cold water, a little at a time, and mix to a firm dough. Knead the dough on a flat surface for 4-5 minutes. Cover with a damp cloth or wrap in plastic wrap. Leave to stand at room temperature for 30-40 minutes. Roll out on a well-floured surface as thinly as possible, until almost transparent. Cut into round or square pieces to suit your requirements. Use the wrappers within a few hours of making otherwise they will dry out.

MAKES: 40-50

Wontons with Pork and Shrimp Filling

Chinese hors d'oeuvres are variations on a few basic themes. Here is another wonton favorite.

PREPARATION TIME: 30 minutes
COOKING TIME: 10-15 minutes

1½ cups lean ground pork
2 tbsps salad or olive oil
1½ cups peeled small shrimp, finely chopped
3 green onions, finely chopped
½ tsp ground white pepper
1¼ tbsps soy sauce
1½ tsps rice wine or dry sherry
½ tsp salt, or to taste

1½ tsps cornstarch blended with 2 tbsps water
40-50 wonton wrappers
2 tbsps all-purpose flour, mixed with a little cold water to a smooth paste
Oil for deep-frying

Fry the pork in the 2 tbsps oil until it loses its pink color. Add the shrimp and onions and fry for 3-4 minutes. Add the pepper, soy sauce and wine. Season with salt and stir-fry for 1-2 minutes. Add the blended cornstarch and stir over a moderate heat until thickened. Allow to cool before filling the wontons. Divide the filling into 40-50 equal portions. Take a wonton wrapper, moisten the edges with the flour and water paste. Place a portion of filling in the center of each wonton wrapper and gather up the edges to make a neat round, alternatively shape into a triangle or any other shape that you prefer. Once you have shaped all the wontons, deep-fry them in hot oil until crisp and golden. You will need to fry them in 3 or more batches. Drain well on paper towels before serving.

SERVES: 2

Steamed Sea Bass

Steaming is a very healthy cooking method, allowing the food to keep all its goodness and taste.

PREPARATION TIME: 15-20 minutes
COOKING TIME: 20-25 minutes

1 whole fish (about 1½lbs)
2 green onions
1-2 slices bacon

SAUCE AND GARNISH
2 slices fresh ginger root
2 green onions
1½ tbsps soy sauce
1 tbsp pale dry sherry
1½ tbsps oil

Clean and gut the fish. Cut the green onions into 2-inch pieces. Shred the bacon. To prepare the sauce and garnish, cut the ginger and green onions into fine shreds. Mix the soy sauce with the sherry. Place the fish in a heatproof pan. Spoon the green onions, ginger root and bacon shreds along the length of the fish. Insert the dish into a steamer and steam vigorously for 15-20 minutes. Remove the ginger, green onions and bacon from the fish.

Just before serving, pour the soy/sherry mixture over the fish. Garnish with the shredded green onions and ginger. Heat the oil over a high heat until it is about to smoke. Pour the hot oil over the fish, creating a loud sizzle. Serve at once.

The Tian Mountains, the "mountains of heaven," whose snow-capped summits are reminiscent of the Rocky Mountains.

SERVES: 6

Kung Pao Shrimp with Cashew Nuts

This dish was named for a Szechuan governor, whose official title was
"Kung Pao".

PREPARATION TIME: 20 minutes
COOKING TIME: 3 minutes

½ tsp chopped fresh ginger
1 tsp chopped garlic
1½ tbsps cornstarch
¼ tsp baking soda
Salt and pepper
¼ tsp sugar
1lb uncooked shrimp
4 tbsps oil
1 small onion, cut into dice
1 large or 2 small zucchini, cut
  into ½-inch cubes

1 small red pepper, cut into ½-inch
  cubes
½ cup cashew nuts

SAUCE
¾ cup chicken stock
1 tbsp cornstarch
2 tsps chili sauce
2 tsps bean paste (optional)
2 tsps sesame oil
1 tbsp dry sherry or rice wine

Mix together the ginger, garlic, 1½ tbsps cornstarch, baking soda, salt, pepper and
sugar. If the shrimp are unpeeled, remove the shells and the dark vein running along
the back of the shrimp. If the shrimp are large, cut them in half. Place in the dry
ingredients and leave to stand for 20 minutes.

Heat the oil in a wok and when hot, add the shrimp. Cook, stirring, over a high
heat for about 20 seconds, or just until the shrimp change color. Transfer to a plate.
Add the onion to the same oil in the wok and cook for about 1 minute. Add the
zucchini and red pepper and cook about 30 seconds.

Mix the sauce ingredients together and add to the wok. Cook, stirring constantly,
until the sauce is slightly thickened. Add the shrimp and the cashew nuts and heat
through completely. Serve immediately.

*The Ancestor Worshipping Cave at Luoyang on the west bank of
the Li River in Honan province contains some of the finest rock
carvings in China.*

SERVES: 3-4

Fish in Wine Sauce

The cloud ear fungus is a traditional ingredient in this dish, but can be replaced with other dried Chinese mushrooms, if it proves difficult to find.

PREPARATION TIME: 20 minutes
COOKING TIME: 15 minutes

MARINADE
¼ tsp salt
1 egg white
2 tsps cornstarch
1 tsp wine-flavored vinegar

10-12oz mullet or carp fillet, cut
　into 2-inch slices
Oil for deep-frying
1 cup chicken broth

SEASONING
Pinch monosodium glutamate
　(optional)
Pinch salt
Pinch freshly ground black pepper
1 tsp fine granulated sugar
2½ tsps cornstarch
1½ tbsps water
1 cloud ear fungus, soaked and
　boiled for 2 minutes, and then
　chopped
2 dried Chinese mushrooms,
　soaked and sliced

Mix the marinade ingredients together. Marinate the fish in this mixture for 10 minutes. Heat a generous quantity of oil in the wok and deep-fry the drained fish pieces, a few at a time, until the flesh is white. Remove and drain the fish. Keep the oil for future use. Clean the wok. Add the chicken broth to the wok and bring to the boil. Simmer gently and stir in the seasoning ingredients. Simmer for few seconds and then add the cornstarch blended with the water. Add the fish and simmer until the sauce thickens. Add the fungus and mushrooms. Simmer for 1 minute. Serve immediately.

Encrusted in snow, the famous pines of Mount Huang (facing page) in Anhwei are difficult to distinguish from the peaks themselves.

SERVES: 2

Sweet-Sour Fish

In China this dish is almost always prepared with freshwater fish, but sea bass is also an excellent choice.

PREPARATION TIME: 25 minutes
COOKING TIME: 15-25 minutes

---

1 sea bass, gray mullet or carp,
    weighing about 2lbs, cleaned
1 tbsp dry sherry
Few slices fresh ginger root
½ cup sugar
6 tbsps cider vinegar
1 tbsp soy sauce

2 tbsps cornstarch
1 clove garlic, crushed
2 green onions, shredded
1 small carrot, peeled and finely
    shredded
1oz bamboo shoots, shredded

Rinse the fish well inside and out. Make three diagonal cuts on each side of the fish with a sharp knife. Trim off the fins, leaving the dorsal fin on top. Trim the tail to two neat points.

Bring enough water to cover the fish to the boil in a wok. Gently lower the fish into the boiling water and add the sherry and ginger. Cover the wok tightly and remove at once from the heat. Allow to stand 15-20 minutes to let the fish cook in the residual heat.

To test if the fish is cooked, pull the dorsal fin – if it comes off easily the fish is done. If not, return the wok to the heat and bring to the boil. Remove from the heat and leave the fish to stand a further 5 minutes. Transfer the fish to a heated serving dish and keep it warm. Take all but 4 tbsps of the fish cooking liquid from the wok. Add the remaining ingredients including the vegetables and cook, stirring constantly, until the sauce thickens. Spoon some of the sauce over the fish to serve and serve the rest separately.

Chenyang Bridge, north of Guilin, is constructed almost entirely of wood, without a single nail. It took eleven years to complete.

SERVES: 6

Quick-Fry "Crystal Shrimp"

Serve this quickly-prepared dish as part of a large spread – its simplicity
complements richer dishes to perfection.

PREPARATION TIME: 10 minutes
COOKING TIME: 5 minutes

1lb fresh shrimp	2 tsps chopped onion
1 egg white	½ tsp salt
1 tbsp cornstarch	1 tbsp pale dry sherry
6 tbsps oil	2 tbsps chicken broth
1 tsp chopped fresh ginger root	½ tbsp vinegar

Clean, shell and devein the shrimp. Mix together the egg white and cornstarch. Toss
the shrimp in this mixture to coat well. Heat the oil in a wok. Add the shrimp. Stir-fry
over a low heat for 2-3 minutes until turning color. Remove with a slotted spoon. Pour
off any excess oil. Add the chopped ginger, onion, salt, sherry, and broth. Bring to the
boil. Return the shrimp to the wok. Stir over the heat for a few seconds. Sprinkle with
vinegar. Serve.

*Facing page: Dragon Gate on the Western Hills in Yünnan
province affords a magnificent, if vertiginous, view of Lake Dian.*

SERVES: 6

Singapore Fish

The cuisine of Singapore was much influenced by that of China. In turn, the Chinese have brought ingredients like curry powder into their own cuisine.

PREPARATION TIME: 25 minutes
COOKING TIME: 10 minutes

1lb whitefish fillets
1 egg white
1 tbsp cornstarch
2 tsps white wine
Salt and pepper
Oil for frying
1 large onion, cut into ½-inch-thick wedges
1 tbsp mild curry powder

1 small can pineapple pieces, drained and juice reserved, or ½ fresh pineapple, peeled and cubed
1 small can mandarin orange segments, drained and juice reserved
1 small can sliced water chestnuts, drained
1 tbsp cornstarch mixed with juice of 1 lime
2 tsps sugar (optional)
Pinch salt and pepper

Starting at the tail end of the fillets, skin them using a sharp knife. Slide the knife back and forth along the length of each fillet, pushing the fish flesh along as you go. Cut the flesh into even-sized pieces, about 2 inches square.

Mix together the egg white, cornstarch, wine, salt and pepper. Place the fish in the mixture and leave to stand while heating the oil. When the oil is hot, fry a few pieces of fish at a time until light golden brown and crisp. Remove the fish to paper towels to drain, and continue until all the fish is cooked.

Remove all but 1 tbsp of the oil from the wok and add the onion. Stir-fry the onion for 1-2 minutes and add the curry powder. Cook the onion and curry powder for a further 1-2 minutes. Add the juice from the pineapple and the mandarin oranges and bring to the boil. Combine the cornstarch and lime juice and add a spoonful of the boiling fruit juice. Return the mixture to the wok and cook until thickened, about 2 minutes. Taste and add sugar if desired. Add the fruit, water chestnuts and fried fish to the wok and stir to coat. Heat through 1 minute and serve immediately.

The sun highlights a restored section of the Great Wall of China at Badaling, northwest of Peking.

The sixth-century Longxing Monastery at Zhengding in Hopeh province is famous for its huge bronze Buddha, which is over sixty feet high and has forty-two arms.

SERVES: 4

Cantonese Prawns

Try eating this dish Western style, with French bread and a salad, for a delicious light lunch.

PREPARATION TIME: 10 minutes
COOKING TIME: 15 minutes

---

3 tbsps salad or olive oil
2 cloves garlic, finely crushed
1lb peeled medium shrimp
2-inch piece fresh root ginger, peeled and finely chopped
1 cup uncooked pork or bacon, finely chopped

SAUCE
1¼ tbsps rice wine or dry sherry

1¼ tbsps light soy sauce
1 tsp fine granulated sugar
1 cup broth or water
1 tbsp cornstarch mixed with 2 tbsps broth or water

2-3 green onions, chopped
2 eggs, lightly beaten

Heat 1 tbsp of the oil in a wok. Add the garlic and fry for 1 minute. Add the shrimp and stir-fry for 4-5 minutes. Remove to a dish and keep warm. Add the remaining oil to the wok and fry the ginger and pork for 3-4 minutes until the meat loses its pink color. Mix together the sauce ingredients, add to the wok and cook for 1 minute. Add the onions and cook for 1 more minute. Add the beaten eggs and cook for 1-2 minutes, without stirring, until set. Spoon the egg mixture over the shrimp. Alternatively, add the shrimp along with the beaten eggs. Allow the eggs to set and then mix gently. Serve at once.

SERVES: 4

Cantonese Ginger and Onion Lobster

This mildly-flavored dish makes a luxurious appetizer.

PREPARATION TIME: 30 minutes
COOKING TIME: 6-7 minutes

1½lb lobster (live)
4 slices ginger root
3 green onions
Oil for deep-frying

½ tsp salt
½ cup chicken stock
1½ tbsps soy sauce
2 tbsps pale dry sherry

Split the lobster in half through the head and tail along the center line of the shell. Discard the grey sac in the head and the dark intestinal vein in the body. Chop into large, bite-sized pieces. Shred the ginger and chop the green onions.

Heat the oil in a deep frying pan. When hot, add the lobster and cook, stirring, for 3 minutes. Add ginger and green onions and salt. Cook for a further minute. Pour off the oil. Add the stock, soy sauce and sherry. Simmer for 3-4 minutes, stirring all the time. Transfer the lobster to a deep-sided serving dish. Pour the contents of the pan over the lobster and serve.

Dating from the eleventh century and standing two hundred and twenty feet high, the Xijia Pagoda at Yingxian is the world's oldest and highest wooden building.

SERVES: 6

Szechuan Fish

The piquant spiciness of Szechuan pepper is quite different from that of black or white pepper. Beware, though, too much can numb the mouth temporarily!

PREPARATION TIME: 30 minutes, plus 4 hours soaking for garnish
COOKING TIME: 10 minutes

Chili peppers, to garnish
1lb whitefish fillets
Pinch salt and pepper
1 egg
5 tbsps flour
6 tbsps white wine
Oil for frying
2oz cooked ham, cut in small dice
1-inch piece fresh ginger, finely diced
½-1 red or green chili pepper, cored, seeded and finely diced

6 water chestnuts, finely diced
4 green onions, finely chopped
3 tbsps light soy sauce
1 tsp cider vinegar or rice wine vinegar
½ tsp ground Szechuan pepper (optional)
1 cup light stock
1 tbsp cornstarch dissolved in 2 tbsps water
2 tsps sugar

To prepare the garnish, choose unblemished chili peppers with the stems on. Using a small, sharp knife, cut the peppers into strips, starting from the pointed end. Cut down to within ½ inch of the stem end. Rinse out the seeds under cold running water and place the peppers in iced water. Leave the peppers to soak for at least 4 hours or overnight until they open up like flowers.

Cut the fish fillets into 2-inch pieces and season with salt and pepper. Beat the egg well and add the flour and wine to make a batter. Dredge the fish lightly with flour and then dip into the batter. Mix the fish well. Heat a wok and when hot, add enough oil to deep-fry the fish. When the oil is hot, fry a few pieces of fish at a time, until golden brown. Drain and proceed until all the fish is cooked.

Remove all but 1 tbsp of oil from the wok and add the ham, ginger, diced chili pepper, water chestnuts and green onions. Cook for about 1 minute and add the soy sauce and vinegar. If using Szechuan pepper, add at this point. Stir well and cook for a further 1 minute. Remove the vegetables from the pan and set them aside. Add the stock to the wok and bring to the boil. When boiling, add 1 spoonful of the hot stock to the cornstarch mixture. Add the mixture back to the stock and reboil, stirring constantly until thickened. Stir in the sugar and return the fish and vegetables to the sauce. Heat through for 30 seconds and serve at once.

For centuries the strangely shaped, jagged peaks of Mount Huang have been a source of inspiration for poets and artists.

Steamed Pork with Ground Rice

Marinating the meat gives piquancy to an otherwise simple dish.

PREPARATION TIME: 10 minutes, plus 20 minutes marinating time
COOKING TIME: 25-30 minutes

1½lbs pork tenderloin
1 tsp salt
2 tbsps soy sauce
2 tbsps Szechuan chili bean paste
1 tsp sugar
3 slices fresh ginger root, finely shredded

4 green onions, finely chopped
Freshly ground Szechuan pepper
1 tbsp oil
4 tbsps ground rice
1 lettuce or cabbage
Sesame oil to garnish

Cut the pork into bite-sized pieces. Marinate in the salt, soy sauce, chili bean paste, sugar, ginger root, green onions, Szechuan pepper and oil, for 20 minutes. Drain and coat each piece of pork with ground rice and arrange in neat layers on a bed of lettuce or cabbage in a steamer and steam vigorously for 25-30 minutes. Garnish with sesame oil, and more finely chopped green onions. Serve with chili sauce as a dip if desired.

*The Pagoda of the 10,000 Buddhas in Gyantse, Tibet, is capped
with gold. The eyes of the Buddha look down from all four sides,
symbolic of his knowledge of all mankind.*

SERVES: 4

Stir-fried Beef with Oyster Sauce

Beef is more popular in Cantonese cooking than elsewhere in China and this particular combination is a regional classic.

PREPARATION TIME: 5 minutes, plus marinating time
COOKING TIME: 20-25 minutes

¾lb lean beef

MARINADE
2 tsps white wine
1 tbsp soy sauce
½ tsp salt
1 tsp sugar
¼ tsp baking powder
¼ tsp pepper
1 tbsp water

2 tsps cornstarch
2 tbsps oil

1 cup broccoli
2 cups oil
2 tbsps oyster sauce
½ tsp salt
1 tsp sugar
2 tsps chopped green onions

Cut the beef into thin 1-inch squares. Mix together all the marinade ingredients, stir in the beef and leave to marinate for several hours. Cook the broccoli in boiling salted water for 15-20 minutes. Drain. Heat the 2 cups oil in a wok, and stir-fry the marinated beef for 20 seconds. Remove the beef with a slotted spoon. Remove all but 4 tbsps oil from the wok. Stir-fry the broccoli for 30 seconds. Add the beef, sprinkle with the oyster sauce, salt, sugar, and chopped green onions. Stir-fry for a further 30 seconds. Serve.

Herds of horses, sheep, and cattle graze on the grasslands of the Inner Mongolian prairie.

SERVES: 4

Szechuan "Yu Hsiang" Pork Ribbons Quick Fried with Shredded Vegetables

This quickly-prepared dish makes a perfect supper in a hurry.

PREPARATION TIME: 20 minutes
COOKING TIME: 8 minutes

¾lb lean pork
3 slices ginger root
2 cloves garlic
¼ cup Szechuan Hot Ja Chai
   pickle
1 cup snow peas
1 cup white cabbage
1 red pepper
2 young carrots
2 dried chili peppers

1 cup bean sprouts
4 tbsps oil
1 tsp salt
3 tsps sesame oil
4 tbsps broth

SAUCE
3 tbsps soy sauce
2 tbsps hoisin sauce
1 tbsp chili sauce
2 tbsps vinegar

Cut pork into very thin slices. Cut again into 1-inch strips. Cut ginger, garlic, pickle, snow peas, cabbage, pepper, carrots and chilies into small slices. Mix together the sauce ingredients.

Heat the 4 tbsps oil in a wok. When hot, add the chilies, pickle, pork and ginger. Stir over a high heat for 2 minutes. Add all the shredded vegetables and bean sprouts. Sprinkle with salt, stir over the heat for 2 minutes. Add the broth, stir for 2 minutes more. Add the sauce ingredients, and sesame oil, stirring for a further 2 minutes.

Serve on a well-heated platter with steamed rice.

Facing page: stone carvings on Gu Mountain in Fuzhou, the capital city of Fukien province.

SERVES: 6

Beef with Tomato & Pepper in Black Bean Sauce

Black beans are a specialty of Cantonese cooking and give a pungent, salty taste to stir-fried dishes.

PREPARATION TIME: 25 minutes
COOKING TIME: 5 minutes

2 large tomatoes
2 tbsps salted black beans
2 tbsps water
4 tbsps dark soy sauce
1 tbsp cornstarch
1 tbsp dry sherry
1 tsp sugar

1lb rump steak, cut into thin strips
1 small green pepper, seeded and
    cored
4 tbsps oil
¾ cup beef stock
Pinch pepper

Core the tomatoes and cut them into 16 wedges. Crush the black beans, add the water and set aside. Combine the soy sauce, cornstarch, sherry, sugar and meat in a bowl and set aside.

Cut the pepper into ½-inch diagonal pieces. Heat the wok and add the oil. When hot, stir-fry the green pepper pieces for about 1 minute and remove. Add the meat and the soy sauce mixture to the wok and stir-fry for about 2 minutes. Add the soaked black beans and the stock. Bring to the boil and allow to thicken slightly. Return the peppers to the wok and add the tomatoes and pepper. Heat through for 1 minute and serve immediately.

Above: the Suzhou River, one of Shanghai's two waterways.
Facing page top left: Lanzhou, the capital of Kansu province
on the Huange River. Facing page top right: the thundering
waters of a breathtaking waterfall in Luoping County.

SERVES: 4

Mu Shu Rou

Mu Shu is Chinese for golden needles, which are the traditional ingredient of this pork dish.

PREPARATION TIME: 30 minutes, in total
COOKING TIME: 10 minutes

½lb ground pork
3 tsps soy sauce
2 tsps water
Salt and pepper
2 tbsps "wooden ears"
2 stalks "golden needles"
4 dried Chinese mushrooms

3 green onions
2 slices fresh ginger root
3 eggs
1 tsp salt
5 tbsps oil
1 tbsp pale dry sherry

Mix the pork with the soy sauce, water, salt and pepper. Marinate for 10 minutes. Drain. Soak all the mushrooms in water for 15 minutes. Drain and shred. Shred the green onions, and ginger. Beat the eggs and the salt. Heat half the oil in a large frying pan. Add the mushrooms and ginger, and stir over the heat for 1 minute. Add the pork, and stir over the heat for 2 minutes. Add the green onions, stir and remove all the contents of the pan with a slotted spoon. Add the remaining oil to the pan. When hot pour in the beaten eggs. When the eggs have set, return the removed contents to the pan. Stir to mix with the egg. Sprinkle with sesame oil and sherry.

Serve wrapped in pancakes, or leaves of crisp lettuce.

The Palace of the Dalai Lama dominates Lhasa, the capital of Tibet.

SERVES: 2-4

Sweet & Sour Pork

This really needs no introduction because of its popularity. The dish originated in Canton, but is reproduced in most of the world's Chinese restaurants.

PREPARATION TIME: 15 minutes
COOKING TIME: 15 minutes

1 cup all-purpose flour
4 tbsps cornstarch
1½ tsps baking powder
Pinch salt
1 tbsp oil
Water
8oz pork tenderloin, cut into
½-inch cubes

SWEET AND SOUR SAUCE
2 tbsps cornstarch
½ cup light brown sugar
Pinch salt
½ cup cider vinegar or rice vinegar
1 clove garlic, crushed
1 tsp grated fresh ginger
6 tbsps tomato ketchup
6 tbsps reserved pineapple juice

1 onion, sliced
1 green pepper, seeded, cored and
sliced
1 small can pineapple chunks,
juice reserved
Oil for frying

To prepare the batter, sift the flour, cornstarch, baking powder and salt into a bowl. Make a well in the center and add the oil and enough water to make a thick, smooth batter. Using a wooden spoon, stir the ingredients in the well, gradually incorporating the flour from the outside, and beat until smooth.

Heat enough oil in a wok to deep-fry the pork. Dip the pork cubes one at a time into the batter and drop into the hot oil. Fry 4-5 pieces of pork at a time and remove them with a draining spoon to paper towels. Continue until all the pork is fried. Pour off most of the oil from the wok and add the sliced onion, pepper and pineapple. Cook over a high heat for 1-2 minutes. Remove and set aside.

Mix all the sauce ingredients together and pour into the wok. Bring slowly to the boil, stirring continuously until thickened. Allow to simmer for about 1-2 minutes or until completely clear. Return the vegetables, pineapple and pork cubes to the sauce and stir to coat completely. Reheat for 1-2 minutes and serve immediately.

Blue-toned mists in the beautiful countryside around Yangshuo, a tiny country town whose name means Bright Moon.

SERVES: 2

Stir-fry Beef with Mango Slices

Mangoes are plentiful in Southern China and add both sweetness and richness to this popular dish.

PREPARATION TIME: 10 minutes, plus 20 minutes marinating time
COOKING TIME: 2-3 minutes

½lb fillet of beef
1 large mango
4 tbsps oil
1 tbsp shredded fresh ginger root
1 tbsp shredded green onions

MARINADE
1 tbsp cooking wine
1 tbsp soy sauce
1 tsp cornstarch
¼ tsp sugar
¼ tsp pepper

Cut the beef into thin bite-sized slices. Mix together the marinade ingredients, stir in the sliced beef and leave to marinate for 20 minutes. Skin the mango, cut into ¼-inch thick slices. Set a wok over a high heat, pour the oil into the wok, and wait until it's almost smoking. Reduce heat to moderate, and stir-fry the drained beef and the ginger for 1-2 minutes. Remove with a slotted spoon. Toss the mango slices in the hot oil for a few seconds, return the beef and ginger, and add the green onions. Stir over the heat for a further few seconds. Serve immediately.

Facing page: Black Dragon Pool Park in Lijang, Yünnan province, contains a pavilion and a Ming Dynasty temple.

SERVES: 4-6

Shanghai Spareribs

These spareribs are so delicious, you'll forget they're a bit messy to eat.

PREPARATION TIME: 5 minutes, plus 3-4 hours marinating time
COOKING TIME: 60-80 minutes

2lbs pork spareribs

MARINADE
¼ cup soy sauce
2 tbsps sugar
2 tbsps hoisin sauce

2 tbsps pale dry sherry
1 tsp garlic, minced
Pepper
Ground ginger
2 tbsps chicken stock or water

Place the spareribs in a large, shallow ovenproof pan. In a small bowl mix all the other ingredients together. Pour this over the spareribs and marinate for 3-4 hours. Turn and baste every hour or so. Cover the pan tightly with foil. Cook at 375° for 45 mins. Uncover, baste ribs with the sauce, and raise the oven temperature to 425°. Cook for a further 15-20 minutes.

Baste and turn occasionally until dark brown. Serve.

The Round City in Peking's Beihai Park.

SERVES: 8

Peking Beef

In China, meat is often simmered in large earthenware casseroles placed on asbestos mats. A wok is a convenient substitute and the stand does the work of the traditional mat.

PREPARATION TIME: 25 minutes
COOKING TIME: 1½ hours

2lb sirloin tip or rump roast
1½ cups white wine
2 cups water
2 whole green onions, roots
   trimmed
1-inch piece fresh ginger

3 star anise
2 tsps sugar
½ cup soy sauce
1 carrot, peeled
2 sticks celery
½ mooli (daikon) radish, peeled

Place the beef in a wok and add the white wine, water, green onions, ginger and star anise. Cover and simmer for about 1 hour. Add the sugar and soy sauce, stir and simmer for 30 minutes longer, or until the beef is tender. Allow to cool in the liquid.

Shred all the vegetables finely. Blanch them in boiling water for about 1 minute. Rinse under cold water, drain and leave to dry. When the meat is cold, remove it from the liquid and cut into thin slices. Arrange them on a serving plate and strain the liquid over. Scatter over the shredded vegetables and serve cold.

This huge bronze buddha is over sixty feet high and was cast in 971.

SERVES: 6

Lion's Head

A classic dish from Yang Chow, Lion's Head has a glossy sauce
of reduced chicken broth.

PREPARATION TIME: 10 minutes
COOKING TIME: 30-40 minutes

2lbs ground pork butt
2 green onions, finely chopped
2 slices fresh ginger root, finely
    chopped
2 tbsps pale dry sherry

2 tbsps cornstarch
1 tbsp lard
1lb Chinese cabbage (bok choy),
    quartered lengthwise
1 cup chicken broth

Mix together the pork, green onions, ginger, sherry, cornstarch, and half the salt.
Shape the mixture into six or eight meatballs. Melt the lard in a deep, flameproof pan.
Add the cabbage and remaining salt, and fry for 30 seconds. Place the meatballs on the
cabbage and pour the broth over the top. Bring to the boil, then cover tightly. Simmer
gently for 30-40 minutes. Serve hot. (Alternatively the meatballs may be fried in a
little lard, with soy sauce and sugar, before placing them on top of the cabbage.)

*Coiling Dragon Ridge on Huashan Mountain, a sacred peak in
Shensi province.*

SERVES: 4

Steamed Beef Szechuan Style

This dish makes a good introduction to Szechuan cooking, being not too fierily spiced.

PREPARATION TIME: 40 minutes
COOKING TIME: 15 minutes

---

3 slices fresh root ginger, minced
1 tsp salt
1 tsp fine granulated sugar
Freshly ground black pepper
1 tbsp salad or olive oil
2 tbsps rice wine or dry sherry
1½ tbsps chili bean paste

2½ tbsps dark soy sauce
3-4 green onions, finely chopped
1lb fillet of beef, cut into 2-inch-long strips
⅔ cup ground rice
1 large lotus leaf or several cabbage leaves

For the marinade, mix the ginger, salt, sugar, pepper, oil, wine, bean paste, soy sauce and half of the onions. Add the beef strips and mix well. Leave to marinate for 15-20 minutes. Heat the wok and dry roast the ground rice for 2-4 minutes till the rice changes color from white to light brown. Roll the marinated beef in the roasted ground rice to give a thin, even coating. Line the bamboo steamer with a well-oiled lotus leaf or a few old and tough cabbage leaves. Arrange the coated beef strips in a neat pile on top. Steam fairly quickly for 10-15 minutes over boiling water. Garnish with the remaining chopped onions before serving. Serve hot with chili sauce.

Facing page: at over 200 feet high, Huangguoshu Falls are the largest in China and the pride of Kweichow province.

SERVES: 4

Braised Hong Kong Beef

Chinese influences show in the use of stir-frying and five-spice powder in this dish.

PREPARATION TIME: 30 minutes
COOKING TIME: 15-17 minutes

---

2 tbsps salad or olive oil
1lb fillet of beef, sliced into
    matchstick-sized strips
1 onion, peeled and sliced
1-inch piece fresh root ginger,
    peeled and cut into thin strips
3-4 fresh tomatoes, cut into thin
    wedges

½lb carrots, scraped and cut into
    2-inch sticks
2½ tsps brown sugar
½ tsp five-spice powder
2¼ tbsps light soy sauce
1 tbsp rice wine or dry sherry
2 tbsps water
Salt to taste

Heat the oil in a wok and fry the beef for 3-4 minutes. Add the onion, ginger, tomatoes and carrots. Stir-fry for 2-3 minutes. Add the sugar, five-spice powder, soy sauce, wine and water. Season with salt to taste and cook gently for 8-10 minutes. Serve immediately.

SERVES: 4

Mongolian Lamb with Onions

The Mongolian influence shows itself in the many lamb dishes of Northern China, where that meat is more popular than anywhere else in the country.

PREPARATION TIME: 20 minutes
COOKING TIME: 8-10 minutes

1lb lean, boned lamb, cut into
    ¼×2-inch strips
1 egg white
2 cloves of garlic, sliced
½ tsp five-spice powder
½-inch piece fresh root ginger,
    peeled and thinly sliced

1 tbsp cornstarch
1¼ tbsps light soy sauce
3½ tbsps rice wine or dry sherry
2 tbsps water
3 tbsps cooked oil
6 green onions, chopped

Mix the lamb with the egg white, garlic, five-spice powder, ginger root and 1 tsp each of the cornstarch and soy sauce. Keep on one side. Mix the remaining cornstarch, soy sauce, wine and water together. Heat the wok and add the oil. When it begins to smoke, add the lamb mixture. Reduce the heat and stir-fry for 3-4 minutes until the meat browns slightly. Remove and keep on one side. Add the onions and the cornstarch, soy sauce and wine mixture to the wok. Stir until it thickens. Return the meat to the wok and simmer gently for 3-4 minutes, or until the meat is tender. Serve as a main dish.

*Top: the three buddhist pagodas at Dali form distinctive
silhouettes against the setting sun. Above left: Braised Hong Kong
Beef. Above right: Mongolian Lamb with Onions*

SERVES: 6

Shanghai Long-cooked Knuckle of Pork

This dish is typical of Eastern cuisine, with its slightly sweet taste.

PREPARATION TIME: 15 minutes
COOKING TIME: COOKING TIME: 2½-3 hours, in total

3-4lb pork hock
7½ cups water
3 green onions
½ cup soy sauce

¼ cup sugar
½ cup pale dry sherry
4 slices fresh ginger root
2 tbsps lard

Clean the pork, and slash with a knife to ease cooking. Place in a deep pan, and add the water. Bring to a boil, then simmer for 15 minutes. Discard ⅓ of the water. Cut the green onions into 1-inch sections. Add the green onions, soy sauce, sugar, sherry, ginger and lard to the pork. Cover and simmer for 2 hours. Turn the pork over several times during cooking. By the end of the cooking time the water in the pan should have reduced to a ¼. Bring to a boil to reduce again by half. The broth will have become rich and brown. Place the pork in a deep bowl. Pour the broth over. Serve with steamed vegetables and rice.

The beautifully preserved Beiling Tomb is one of the most significant buildings in Shenyang, capital of the Manchus in the fifteenth century.

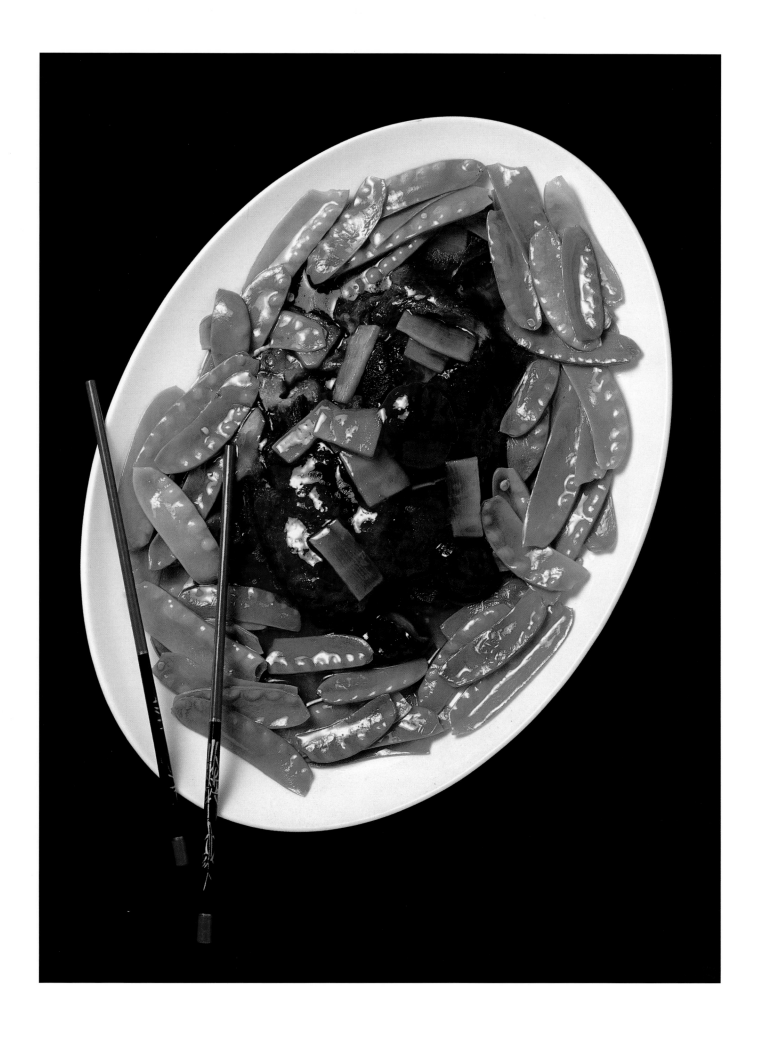

SERVES: 4

Peking Sliced Lamb with Cucumber Soup

This delicate-tasting dish is another lamb specialty from Northern Chinese cuisine.

½lb leg of lamb, boned
5-inch piece cucumber
1 tbsp soy sauce
1½ tsps sesame oil

5 cups chicken broth
Salt and pepper
1½ tbsps wine vinegar

Cut the lamb into wafer-thin slices. Thinly slice the cucumber. Sprinkle the lamb with the soy sauce and sesame oil. Marinate for 15 minutes.

Season the broth with salt and pepper. Bring to a boil. Add the sliced lamb. Poach in the broth for 1 minute. Remove with a slotted spoon. Poach the cucumber in the broth for 2 minutes. Return the lamb, stir in the vinegar, adjust seasoning and serve.

Facing page: Tianchi Lake lies at the foot of Bogda Feng, the highest peak in the spectacular Tian Mountains.

SERVES: 4

Chicken Chop Suey

Chop Suey is a corruption of the Cantonese words for odds and ends and
the dish was invented by Chinese immigrants to make use of available
ingredients in their new homeland.

PREPARATION TIME: 30 minutes
COOKING TIME: 15 minutes

2½ tbsps light soy sauce
1 tsp brown sugar
Salt to taste
1lb boned chicken, cut into 1-inch
    pieces
2 tbsps salad or olive oil
1 onion, cut into chunks

2½ cups bean sprouts
2 tsps sesame oil
¼ tsp monosodium glutamate
    (optional)
1 tbsp cornstarch
1 cup chicken broth

Mix the soy sauce with the sugar and salt and add the chicken pieces. Allow to
marinate for 5 minutes. Drain the chicken and reserve the marinade. Heat the wok
and add the oil. Fry the chicken for 2-3 minutes. Remove the chicken. Fry the onions
for 2-3 minutes and add the bean sprouts. Stir-fry for 4-5 minutes. Return the chicken
to the pan and add the sesame oil. Dissolve the monosodium glutamate and the
cornstarch in the broth and pour over the chicken mixture. Cook for 2-3 minutes,
stirring, until the sauce thickens. Serve over rice.

*Facing page: a precarious path descends the rocky face of Mount
Fengkuang, northwest of Dandong.*

SERVES: 4

Tangerine Peel Chicken

Dried tangerine peel is a favorite Chinese ingredient and adds its special tang to this traditional dish.

PREPARATION TIME: 30 minutes
COOKING TIME: 12-15 minutes

1lb boned chicken breast, cut into 1-inch pieces

SEASONING
½ tsp salt
1½ tsps brown sugar
½ tsp monosodium glutamate (optional)
1 tsp dark soy sauce
2½ tsps light soy sauce
1 tsp rice wine or dry sherry
2½ tsps brown vinegar
1 tsp sesame oil
2 tsps cornstarch

Oil for deep-frying
1-2 red or green chilies, chopped
½-inch piece fresh root ginger, peeled and finely chopped
2 inches dried tangerine peel, coarsely ground or crumbled
2 green onions, finely chopped

SAUCE
½ tsp cornstarch
1-2 tbsps water or broth

Mix the chicken pieces with the seasoning ingredients and stir together well. Leave to marinate for 10-15 minutes. Remove the chicken pieces and reserve the marinade. Heat a wok and add the oil for deep-frying. Once it starts to smoke, add the chicken pieces and fry for 4-5 minutes until golden. Drain the chicken on kitchen paper. Tip off the oil, leaving 1 tbsp oil in the wok, and stir-fry the chilies, ginger, tangerine peel and onions for 2-3 minutes. When they begin to color add the chicken and stir-fry for 1 minute. Mix the reserved marinade with the sauce ingredients and pour over the chicken. Stir and cook for 2-3 minutes until the sauce thickens and the chicken is tender. Serve immediately.

The spectacular view of Jinxui Valley from Dragon Head Cliff on Mount Lu, near the northern border of Kiangsi province.

SERVES: 4-6

The Peking Duck

The best-known dish of Peking cuisine outside China, this is almost a meal in itself.

PREPARATION TIME: 10 minutes, plus overnight standing
COOKING TIME: 1¼ hours

---

1 duck, weighing 4 lbs
½ medium cucumber
4 green onions

SAUCE
Small can yellow bean sauce
3 tbsps sugar
2 tbsps oil

Clean and dry the duck. Leave in a cool place overnight. Finely shred the cucumber and green onions. Preheat the oven to 400°F. Place the duck on a wire range set on top of a baking pan. Cook the duck for 1¼ hours. The duck should be very dark and crispy.

Heat 2 tbsps oil in a small pan. Add the yellow bean paste and sugar. Cook together for 1-2 minutes.

Peel the skin off the duck. Cut into 2-inch slices. Serve on a heated platter. Carve the meat off the duck into 2-inch slices, and serve on a separate platter. The duck skin and meat are eaten by wrapping them in pancakes which are first of all brushed with 1 tsp of sauce and sprinkled with a layer of cucumber and green onion.

MAKES: 16-20 pancakes

Pancakes (Po Ping)

These are the pancakes to serve with that classic dish, Peking Duck.

PREPARATION TIME: 6 minutes
COOKING TIME: 15 minutes

1lb all-purpose flour
Pinch salt
1¼ tbsps salad or olive oil

1 tsp sesame oil
Tepid water for kneading
Flour for rolling

Sift the flour and salt into a mixing bowl. Make a well in the center and add the oils and water, a little at a time, and work in the flour. Make a pliable dough. Remove from the bowl and knead well for 2-3 minutes. Cover with a damp, clean cloth and allow to rest for 10 minutes. Knead again for 1 minute and divide the dough into 16-20 even-sized balls. Roll each ball in flour and roll out into a 4-6 inch circle. Heat a skillet until moderately hot and then place the rolled circle of dough on it; cook for ½-1 minute. Little bubbles will appear; flip over and allow to cook for 1-1½ minutes. Pick the pancake up and check whether little brown specs have appeared on the undersides; if not, then cook for few seconds more. Use a clean kitchen towel to press the pancakes gently, this will circulate the steam and cook the pancakes. Prepare the rest of the pancakes in the same way and keep them stacked, wrapped in foil, to keep them warm.

SERVES: 4

The Hainan "Chicken Rice"

The chicken should be eaten dipped in soy sauce to which has been added some garlic, green onion and sesame oil.

PREPARATION TIME: 15 minutes
COOKING TIME: 1½ hours, in total

1lb long-grain rice
1 chicken, weighing 3lbs
¾lb broccoli
2 medium onions

3 slices ginger root
3 tsps salt
¼lb green peas

Cook the rice in boiling salted water until tender, and drain. Bone the chicken and chop into 3-inch bite-sized pieces. Cut the broccoli into same-sized pieces. Thinly slice the onion.

Simmer the chicken in a large pan with 2½ pints water, the ginger, onion and salt, for about 50 minutes or until the chicken is cooked. Remove the chicken, and skim away the excess fat from the broth. Add the broccoli and peas. Bring to the boil. Stir for a few minutes. Finally add the rice, and leave to cook gently for 5 minutes or until the broth has been absorbed. Arrange the chicken pieces on top of the rice and vegetables. Cover the pan to allow the chicken pieces to heat through.

This captivating manmade lake (facing page) is just outside Shaoxing in Chekiang province. Formed in a quarry of hard green rock by damming hill streams, the water seems emerald in the sun.

SERVES: 4

Peking Egg Battered Chicken with Bean Sprouts, in Onion and Garlic Sauce

A light and nutritious dish, in which the crunch of bean sprouts contrasts well with the tenderness of the chicken.

PREPARATION TIME: 15 minutes
COOKING TIME: 5-6 minutes

---

3 breasts of chicken	4 tbsps oil
Salt and pepper	4 tbsps chicken broth
2 eggs	Vinegar to taste
2 cloves garlic	½lb bean sprouts
2 green onions	

Cut each chicken breast into 4-inch slices. Rub with salt and pepper. Beat the eggs lightly, and add the chicken slices to the eggs. Crush the garlic and cut the green onions into 1-inch pieces. Heat the oil in the wok. Add the chicken pieces one by one, and reduce heat to low. Leave to sauté for 1-2 minutes. Once the eggs have set, sprinkle the chicken with the garlic and green onion. Finally, add the broth, vinegar to taste, and the bean sprouts. Simmer gently for 2 minutes.

Remove the chicken, cut each piece into small even-sized pieces, and serve on a heated platter. Pour the remaining sauce from the pan over the chicken.

Mount Taishan (facing page) is one of China's holy mountains and many grandmothers come here every year to offer prayers for their families.

SERVES: 4

Szechuan Bang Bang Chicken

This is a good dish to serve as an appetizer. The diners should actually toss and mix the ingredients in the dish at the table themselves.

PREPARATION TIME: 15 minutes
COOKING TIME: 30 minutes

---

2 chicken breasts
1 medium cucumber

SAUCE
4 tbsps peanut butter

2 tsps sesame oil
½ tsp sugar
¼ tsp salt
2 tsps chicken broth
½ tsp chili sauce

Simmer the chicken in a pan of water for 30 minutes. Remove the chicken breasts and cut them into ½-inch thick strips. Thinly slice the cucumber. Spread cucumber on a large serving platter. Pile the shredded chicken on top. Mix the peanut butter with the sesame oil, sugar, salt and broth. Pour the sauce evenly over the chicken. Sprinkle the chili sauce evenly over the top.

Mid-water pavilions at the eighteenth-century Imperial Summer Retreat in Chengde, Hopeh province.

SERVES: 4

Chicken with Walnuts & Celery

Oyster sauce lends a subtle, slightly salty taste to this Cantonese dish.

PREPARATION TIME: 20 minutes
COOKING TIME: 8 minutes

8oz boned chicken, cut into 1-inch
   pieces
2 tsps soy sauce
2 tsps brandy
1 tsp cornstarch
Salt and Pepper

2 tbsps oil
1 clove garlic
1 cup walnut halves
3 stick celery, cut in diagonal slices
½ cup water or chicken stock
2 tsps oyster sauce

Combine the chicken with the soy sauce, brandy, cornstarch, salt and pepper.

Heat a wok and add the oil and garlic. Cook for about 1 minute to flavor the oil. Remove the garlic and add the chicken in two batches. Stir-fry quickly without allowing the chicken to brown. Remove the chicken and add the walnuts to the wok. Cook for about 2 minutes until the walnuts are slightly brown and crisp.

Add the sliced celery to the wok and cook for about 1 minute. Add the oyster sauce and water and bring to the boil. When boiling, return the chicken to the pan and stir to coat all the ingredients well. Serve immediately.

Facing page: a Buddhist statue in Roushen Hall on Mount Jiuhua, one of four sacred Buddhist mountains in China.

SERVES: 4

Chicken Chow Mein

This Chinese-American dish takes its name from the Mandarin for fried
noodles, the central ingredient of any Chow Mein.

PREPARATION TIME: 30 minutes
COOKING TIME: 20 minutes

1lb egg noodles or spaghetti,
  broken into small pieces
1 onion, peeled and thinly sliced
½ cup mushrooms, sliced
3 green onions, chopped
2 cloves of garlic, peeled and
  chopped
Salt to taste

Pinch monosodium glutamate
4 tbsps salad or olive oil
1½ cups chicken meat, finely
  shredded
2½ tbsps light soy sauce
1 tsp fine granulated sugar
1 tbsp rice wine or dry sherry
⅓ cup chicken broth

Cook the noodles in boiling, salted water for 4-5 minutes until tender. Drain and rinse
under cold water. Drain once again and add 2 tbsps of the oil; mix well to prevent the
noodles from sticking together and fry gently for a few minutes. Heat the remaining oil
in a wok and fry the onions and garlic for 2 minutes. Add the chicken and stir-fry for
3-4 minutes. Add the mushrooms. Sprinkle over the wine, sugar, soy sauce,
monosodium glutamate and salt to taste. Cook until the mixture is fairly dry. Add the
noodles and stir well to mix. Sprinkle over the broth and cook once again until dry.
Serve with chili sauce and dark soy sauce. ½ cup sliced green beans, ⅓ cup lightly
cooked peas or ⅓ cup shredded carrot may also be added, along with the chicken
pieces.

*The port of Chongqing in Szechuan province has undergone
numerous urban development programs, but parts of the old
town (facing page) still remain.*

SERVES: 6

Yang Chow Fried Rice

Popular throughout China, this dish came originally from the city of the
same name in the Eastern province.

PREPARATION TIME: 10 minutes
COOKING TIME: 6-8 minutes

3 tbsps salad or olive oil
1 egg, beaten
1 cup cooked meat, chopped
  (pork, lamb, beef)
1 cup medium shrimp, shelled and
  chopped

½ cup shelled green peas, lightly
  cooked
2 green onions, chopped
1lb dry, cooked rice
Salt to taste
1 tsp monosodium glutamate
  (optional)

Heat 1 tbsp of the oil in a wok. Fry the beaten egg until set, and break into small
lumps. Remove the egg. Add the remaining oil and fry the meat, shrimp, peas and
onions for 1-2 minutes. Add the cooked rice and sprinkle with salt and monosodium
glutamate. Fry for 3 minutes. Mix in the cooked egg and serve immediately.

*Facing page: the Yellow Crane Tower at Wuhan, Hupeh province,
is a reconstruction of the original third-century tower that was
burned down in 1884.*

SERVES: 4

South Sea Noodles

Although strictly a Chinese "filler", this would also
make a good lunch dish.

PREPARATION TIME: 15 minutes
COOKING TIME: 7-8 minutes

---

2 tbsps Chinese dried shrimp,
   soaked
½lb Chinese rice noodles
4 tbsps oil
2 medium onions, sliced
4 slices bacon
2 tbsps curry powder
Salt
½ cup chicken broth

GARNISH
½lb shelled shrimp
2 cloves garlic, chopped
1 tbsp soy sauce
1 tbsp hoisin sauce
1 tbsp pale dry sherry
2 tbsps oil
4 green onions, chopped
2 tbsps chopped parsley

Drain the dried shrimp, and chop. Cook the noodles in boiling water for 3 minutes,
drain and rinse under cold water. Heat the oil in a wok, add the onion, chopped bacon
and dried shrimp. Stir-fry for 1 minute, then add the curry powder and salt. Fry for a
further 1 minute. Add the broth and noodles. Stir over the heat for 2-3 minutes.
Transfer to a heated serving platter. For the garnish, heat the oil in a small pan, add the
shrimp and garlic and stir-fry over a high heat for 1 minute. Add the soy and hoisin
sauces, and sherry. Sprinkle with green onions and parsley. Pour on top of noodles to
serve.

*The wonderful ceramic beasts of the Nine Dragons Screen in
Peking's Beihai Park were designed to protect a temple from evil
spirits.*

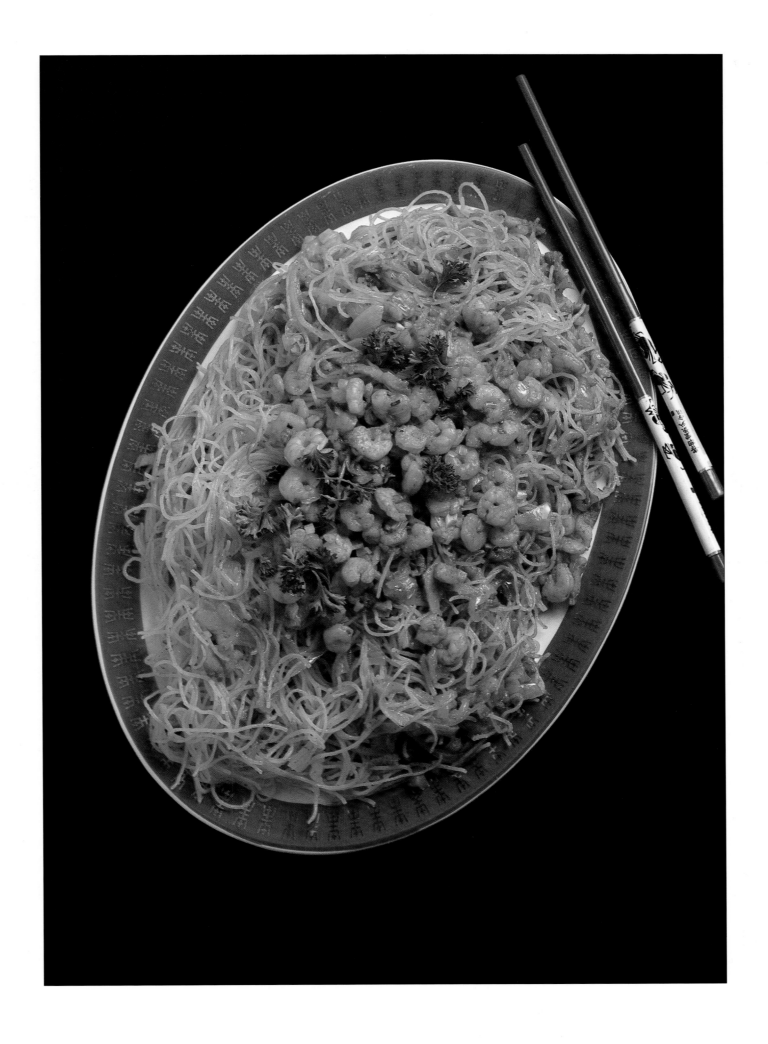

SERVES: 4-6

Noodles in Soup

This dish is very versatile; serve it as a substantial starter, a light meal or an unusual side dish.

PREPARATION TIME: 10 minutes
COOKING TIME: 6-8 minutes

1lb small rounds of cake noodles
Salt
5½ cups chicken or beef broth
1 cup cooked shredded chicken

2 eggs, hard-boiled and sliced
1⅓ cups Chinese napa cabbage, or
    iceberg lettuce, finely shredded
2 green onions, thinly sliced

Cook the noodles in boiling salted water for 5 minutes. Drain thoroughly. Heat the broth and add salt to taste. Serve the cooked noodles in bowls, and pour over the hot broth. Garnish with the chicken, sliced eggs, cabbage and green onions.

SERVES: 4-6

Rice Noodles
Singapore Style

This mild-flavored dish is a complete meal in itself.

PREPARATION TIME: 15 minutes, plus soaking time for noodles
COOKING TIME: about 15 minutes

8oz rice noodles
Salad or olive oil
2 eggs, beaten
½-inch piece fresh root ginger,
    peeled and shredded
1½ cups bean sprouts
1 cup cooked ham, pork or
    chicken, shredded

3 tbsps chives, finely chopped
2 cloves garlic, finely chopped
Salt to taste
2 tbsps chicken broth
3 tbsps soy sauce
3 green onions, chopped

Soak the rice noodles in warm water for 10 minutes and then drain well. Heat 1 tbsp oil in a skillet or wok and fry the beaten eggs to make a thin pancake. Slide onto a plate and cut into thin strips. Heat a wok or skillet and add 1 tbsp oil. Fry the ginger and bean sprouts for 2 minutes. Slide onto a plate. Heat the wok or skillet with a further 1 tbsp oil and fry the pork or chicken and the chives for 1-2 minutes. Slide onto a plate. Heat 2 tbsps oil in the wok or skillet and brown the garlic. Add the rice noodles and stir-fry for 2-3 minutes. Add salt to taste, chicken broth, bean sprouts and the pork or chicken. Mix well, sprinkle with soy sauce and stir over the heat for 1 minute. Top with the strips of egg pancake and chopped green onions and serve immediately.

Top: the beautifully preserved eigth-century Yueyang Tower,
built without nails, at Yueyang, on the Yangtse River. Above
left: Noodles in Soup. Above right: Rice Noodles Singapore Style

SERVES: 6-8

Fried Rice

A basic recipe for a traditional Chinese accompaniment to stir-fried dishes, this can be made more substantial with the addition of meat, poultry or seafood.

PREPARATION TIME: minimal
COOKING TIME: 14 minutes plus 20 minutes draining time

1lb cooked rice, well drained and
    dried
3 tbsps oil
1 egg, beaten
1 tbsp soy sauce

2oz cooked peas
2 green onions, thinly sliced
Dash sesame oil
Salt and pepper

Heat a wok and add the oil. Pour in the egg and soy sauce and cook until just beginning to set. Add the rice and peas and stir to coat with the egg mixture. Allow to cook for about 3 minutes, stirring continuously. Add the sesame oil and season to taste. Spoon into a serving dish and sprinkle over the green onions.

The outcrops of rock on Mount Tianzi (facing page) in Hunan province are home to trees which seem almost as light and feathery as the mists which float around them.

SERVES: 4

Shanghai Noodles

In general, noodles are more popular in northern and eastern China, where wheat is grown, than in other parts of the country. They make a popular snack in Chinese tea houses.

PREPARATION TIME: 10 minutes
COOKING TIME: 6-8 minutes

3 tbsps oil
4oz chicken breast
1lb thick Shanghai noodles
4oz Chinese cabbage

4 green onions, thinly sliced
2 tbsps soy sauce
Freshly ground black pepper
Dash sesame oil

Heat the oil in the wok and add the chicken, cut into thin shreds. Stir-fry for 2-3 minutes. Meanwhile, cook the noodles in boiling salted water until just tender, about 6-8 minutes. Drain in a colander and rinse under hot water. Toss in the colander to drain and leave to dry.

Add the shredded Chinese cabbage and green onions to the chicken in the wok along with the soy sauce, pepper and sesame oil. Cook about 1 minute and toss in the cooked noodles. Stir well and heat through. Serve immediately.

Aiwan Pavilion on Yuela Hill in Changsha was a haunt of Mao Zedong's during his youth and bears a tablet of the Chinese leader's writing.

Sizzling Rice or Singing Rice

When rice is cooked, the crust that forms on the bottom of the pot can be dried and then deep fried. When it is immersed in gravy or soup it makes a sizzling noise, hence the name. Once made or collected, the rice crusts can be kept for months.

PREPARATION TIME: 50 minutes
COOKING TIME: 2 hours, plus time for deep-frying the rice

4oz short grain rice	Oil for frying

Wash the rice in 4-5 changes of water until the water runs clear. Drain the rice and put it into a pan with 1¼ cups of water; bring to the boil. Reduce heat to low and cook for 20 minutes, simmering gently. Turn off the heat and let the rice stand, covered for 25-30 minutes. Take a non-stick skillet and transfer the rice into it. Spread evenly to a thickness of ½ inch. Cook on a very gentle heat for 40-50 minutes. Turn over and cook gently for another hour. The rice should be very dry. Break into 2-inch squares and store in a glass jar with a lid.

To cook sizzling rice, pour oil into a pan to a depth of 2 inches and bring to a moderately high temperature, 375°F. Add the rice squares and fry until golden brown. Remove and drain on paper towels. Serve with soup or any stir-fried dish.

Facing page: three Buddhist pagodas at Dali, the largest of which dates from the Tang dynasty and is over 1,200 years old.

SERVES: 4

Eggplant & Pepper Szechuan Style

Authentic Szechuan food is fiery hot. Outside China, restaurants often tone down the taste for Western palates.

PREPARATION TIME: 30 minutes
COOKING TIME: 7-8 minutes

---

1 large eggplant
Oil for cooking
2 cloves garlic, crushed
1-inch piece fresh ginger, shredded
1 onion, cut into 1-inch pieces
1 small green bell pepper, seeded,
    cored and cut into 1-inch pieces
1 small red bell pepper, seeded,
    cored and cut into 1-inch pieces

1 red or green chili, seeded, cored
    and cut into thin strips
½ cup chicken or vegetable stock
1 tsp sugar
1 tsp vinegar
Pinch salt and pepper
1 tsp cornstarch
1 tbsp soy sauce
Dash sesame oil

Cut the eggplants in half and score the surface. Sprinkle lightly with salt and leave to drain in a colander or on paper towels for 30 minutes. After 30 minutes, squeeze the eggplant gently to extract any bitter juices and rinse thoroughly under cold water. Pat dry and cut the eggplant into 1-inch cubes. Heat about 3 tbsps oil in a wok. Add the eggplant and stir-fry for about 4-5 minutes. It may be necessary to add more oil as the eggplant cooks. Remove from the wok and set aside.

Reheat the wok and add 2 tbsps oil. Add the garlic and ginger and stir-fry for 1 minute. Add the onions and stir-fry for 2 minutes. Add the green pepper, red pepper and chili pepper and stir-fry for 1 minute. Return the eggplant to the wok along with the remaining ingredients. Bring to the boil, stirring constantly, and cook until the sauce thickens and clears. Serve immediately.

The Temple of Heaven marks a sacred spot in Peking where the emperors used to pray for a good harvest.

SERVES: 4

Bamboo Shoots with Green Vegetables

This side dish is particularly good with roast Peking duck.

PREPARATION TIME: 10 minutes
COOKING TIME: 10-12 minutes

Oil for cooking
8oz spinach, or chopped broccoli

SEASONING
½ cup chicken broth or water
¼ tsp monosodium glutamate
   (optional)
¼ tsp salt
¼ tsp fine granulated sugar
1 cup bamboo shoots, sliced

SAUCE
1½ tsps light soy sauce
Pinch monosodium glutamate
1½ tsps cornstarch
3 tsps water
1 tbsp cooked oil

Heat 2 tbsps oil in the wok. Fry the spinach for 2 minutes and add the mixed seasoning ingredients. Simmer for 1 minute and remove from the wok into a dish. Heat the wok and add 1 tbsp oil. Add the bamboo shoots and fry for 1-2 minutes. Return the spinach mixture to the wok. Cook for 3 minutes. Mix together the sauce ingredients. Add to the wok and cook for 1-2 minutes, stirring constantly until thickened.

Tibet is ringed by the world's highest mountains and is a landscape largely free of man's influence. The highest peak in eastern Tibet is Namjagbarwa Feng (facing page) at over 25,000 feet.

MAKES: 6 pancakes
Peking Onion Pancake
Serve this dish as a "filler" with other Chinese dishes.

PREPARATION TIME: 30-35 minutes
COOKING TIME: 6 minutes per pancake

3 cups all-purpose flour
1 cup boiling water
⅓ cup cold water

6 tbsps chopped onion
3 tsps salt
5 tbsps oil

Place the flour in a bowl. Gradually add the boiling water, stirring all the time. Leave for 3 minutes. Stir in the cold water. Knead well. Leave, covered, for 20 minutes. Divide into 6 pieces, roll into 6 large 10-inch pancakes. Sprinkle each with 1 tbsp chopped onion and ½ tsp salt. Tightly roll up each pancake. Twist into a coil. Press flat with palm of hand and roll to ¼-inch thick pancakes. Heat the oil in a large frying pan. Fry the pancakes over a medium heat for 3 minutes on each side. Serve cut into wedges.

A sixth-century Sui Dynasty bridge and buildings on Mount Cangyan in Jingxing County, Hopeh.

Ta'er Monastery near Xining is the most important lamasery outside Tibet, and the current Dalai Lama was born and trained here.

SERVES: 4

Fried Bean Curd with Mushrooms

Although included here as a side dish, the nutritious quality of bean curd means it could equally well be served as a light supper dish on its own.

PREPARATION TIME: 15 minutes
COOKING TIME: 12-15 minutes

8oz large cap mushrooms, sliced

SEASONING
1 tbsp rice wine or dry sherry
2 tsps fine granulated sugar

4 dried Chinese mushrooms,
    soaked and sliced
Pinch baking soda
8oz mustard green or spinach, cut
    into 3-inch pieces

4 squares bean curd (tofu), cubed
1-inch piece fresh root ginger,
    peeled and shredded
2 green onions, chopped
½ cup cooked ham, shredded

SAUCE
1½ tbsps oyster sauce
1½ tbsps dark soy sauce
1½ tbsps cornstarch
6 tbsps broth or water
Freshly ground black pepper

Blanch the fresh mushrooms in water for 1 minute. Drain the mushrooms and discard the water. Mix the seasoning ingredients together and marinate the dried and cap mushrooms for 5-6 minutes. Discard the marinade. Bring 5 cups of water to the boil and add the baking soda and salt. Blanch the greens for 2 minutes. Drain the greens. Discard the water. Sprinkle ½ tsp salt over the bean curd. Deep-fry in hot oil until golden brown. Drain and remove. Heat 2 tbsps oil in the wok and stir-fry the ginger, onions and ham for 2-3 minutes. Return the mushrooms to the wok and mix with the ginger and onions. Add the blended sauce ingredients and bring to a boil. Add the bean curd and simmer until the sauce thickens. Arrange the greens on a dish and pour the sauce over them. Sprinkle with freshly ground black pepper.

SERVES: 2-3

Cantonese Egg Fu Yung

Although this version is from Canton, fu yung dishes are popular in many
other regions of China, too.

PREPARATION TIME: 25 minutes
COOKING TIME: 13 minutes in total

5 eggs
2oz shredded cooked meat, poultry
 or fish
1 stick celery, finely shredded
4 Chinese dried mushrooms,
 soaked in boiling water for
 5 minutes
2oz bean sprouts
1 small onion, thinly sliced
Pinch salt and pepper
1 tsp dry sherry

Oil for frying

SAUCE
1 tbsp cornstarch dissolved in
 3 tbsps cold water
1 cup chicken stock
1 tsp tomato ketchup
1 tbsp soy sauce
Pinch salt and pepper
Dash sesame oil

Beat the eggs lightly and add the shredded meat and celery. Squeeze all the liquid from
the dried mushrooms. Remove the stems and cut the caps into thin slices. Add to the
egg mixture along with the bean sprouts and onion. Add a pinch of salt and pepper
and the sherry and stir well.

Heat a wok or frying pan and pour in about 4 tbsps oil. When hot, carefully spoon
in about ⅓ cup of the egg mixture. Brown on one side, turn gently over and brown the
other side. Remove the cooked patties to a plate and continue until all the mixture is
cooked.

Combine all the sauce ingredients in a small, heavy-based pan and bring slowly to
the boil, stirring continuously until thickened and cleared. Pour the sauce over the egg
patties to serve.

*The Union Tablet is a striking example of urban Revolutionary
sculpture in Yinchuan, capital city of Ninghsia.*

MAKES: 12
Pot Sticker Dumplings

So called because they are fried in very little oil, they will stick unless they
are brown and crisp on the bottom before they are steamed.

PREPARATION TIME: 50 minutes
COOKING TIME: 10-20 minutes

DUMPLING DOUGH
1½ cups all-purpose flour
½ tsp salt
3 tbsps oil
Boiling water

FILLING
4oz finely ground pork or chicken
4 water chestnuts, finely chopped
3 green onions, finely chopped
½ tsp five-spice powder
1 tbsp light soy sauce
1 tsp sugar
1 tsp sesame oil

Sift the flour and salt into a large bowl and make a well in the center. Pour in the oil and add enough boiling water to make a pliable dough. Add about 4 tbsps water at first and begin stirring with a wooden spoon to incorporate the flour gradually. Add more water as necessary. Knead the dough for about 5 minutes and allow to rest for 30 minutes. Divide the dough into 12 pieces and roll each piece out to a circle about 6 inches in diameter.

Mix all the filling ingredients together and place a mound of filling on half of each circle. Fold over the top and press the edges together firmly. Roll over the joined edges using a twisting motion and press down to seal.

Pour about ⅛ inch of oil into a large frying pan, preferably a cast iron one. When the oil is hot, add the dumplings flat side down and cook until nicely browned. When the underside is brown, add about ⅓ cup water to the pan and cover it tightly. Continue cooking gently for about 5 minutes, or until the top surface of dumplings is steamed and appears cooked. Serve immediately.

*Five-Pagoda Temple (facing page) in Hohhot, Mongolia, is a
beautiful building with skilfully carved images of Buddha
repeated all over its facade. The temple is built, exceptionally,
in Classical Indian style.*

SERVES: 4

Ma Po Tou Fu

Bean curd is extremely nutritious but rather bland on its own. In this Szechuan dish it is anything but!

PREPARATION TIME: 30 minutes
COOKING TIME: 14-16 minutes

---

3 cakes bean curd
2 tbsps salted black beans
3 green onions
3 cloves garlic
4 chili peppers
3 tbsps oil

¼lb ground beef
1 tsp salt
1 cup broth
1 tbsp cornstarch
1 tbsp soy sauce
½ tsp pepper

Simmer the bean curd in water for 3 minutes. Drain and cut each cake into a dozen pieces. Soak the black beans in water for 20 minutes. Drain. Chop the green onions, garlic and peppers. Heat the oil in a large wok, and add the beef, salt, and black beans. Stir over the heat for 3-4 minutes. Add the pepper, green onions and garlic. Fry for 2 minutes before adding half the broth, and bean curd. Leave to simmer for 4 minutes.

Mix the remaining broth with the cornstarch and soy sauce. Pour into the wok. Bring to the boil, and simmer for 2-3 minutes. Sprinkle with pepper and serve with rice.

Puji Temple, part of a Buddhist monastery on Puishan Island, off the east coast of Chekiang province.

Calligraphy on a rock face near Taishan Temple on Mount Taishan, one of China's holy mountains.

SERVES: 4-6

Quick-Fried Snow Peas with Bean Sprouts

Don't save this healthy dish just for Chinese meals – serve it as a vegetable side dish any time.

PREPARATION TIME: minimal
COOKING TIME: 4 minutes

¾lb snow peas
1 large piece Szechuan Tsa Chai
   Pickle
4 tbsps oil

1lb bean sprouts
2 tsps salt
2 tsps sesame oil

Finely shred the snow peas and Tsa Chai Pickle. Heat the oil in a large wok. Add the pickle and snow peas. Stir-fry for 2 minutes. Add the bean sprouts, salt and 3 tbsps water. Fry for a further 2 minutes. Sprinkle with sesame oil and serve immediately.

SERVES: 4

Special Mixed Vegetables

This dish illustrates the basic stir-frying technique for vegetables. Use
other varieties for an equally colorful side dish.

PREPARATION TIME: 25 minutes
COOKING TIME: 2½-3 minutes

---

1 tbsp oil
1 clove garlic, crushed
1-inch piece fresh ginger root,
   sliced
4 Chinese cabbage leaves,
   shredded
2oz flat mushrooms, thinly sliced
2oz bamboo shoots, sliced
3 sticks celery, diagonally sliced

2oz baby corn, cut in half if large
1 small red pepper, cored, seeded
   and thinly sliced
2oz bean sprouts
2 tbsps light soy sauce
Dash sesame oil
Salt and pepper
3 tomatoes, peeled

Heat the oil in a wok and add the ingredients in the order given, reserving the
tomatoes until last. Cut the tomatoes in half and then in quarters. Use a teaspoon or a
serrated knife to remove the seeds and the cores. Cook the vegetables for about 2
minutes. Stir in the soy sauce and sesame oil and add the tomatoes. Heat through for
30 seconds and serve immediately.

*A fine bronze ox lies beside the Seventeen-Arched Bridge in the
grounds of Peking's Summer Palace.*

SERVES: 6-8

Coral Cabbage

Red bean-curd cheese, tomato paste and dried shrimp add color and flavor
to this side dish

PREPARATION TIME: 10 minutes
COOKING TIME: 50 minutes, in total

3lbs Chinese cabbage
3 tbsps red bean-curd cheese and
  sauce
2 tbsps tomato paste
1 tbsp light soy sauce
4 tbsps oil

1½ tbsps dried shrimp, soaked and
  chopped
Salt and pepper
2 tbsps butter
1 cup chicken broth

Cut the cabbage into 2-inch pieces. Mix the cheese with the tomato paste, and soy
sauce. Heat the oil in a large wok. Add the shrimp and cabbage. Sprinkle with salt and
pepper. Stir-fry for 1-2 minutes. Add the cheese/soy mixture. Stir the cabbage over the
heat until well coated with sauce. Place in a deep baking pan. Add the butter. Pour the
chicken broth over the vegetables. Cook in a preheated 300°F oven for 45 minutes.
Serve from the pan at the table.

*Facing page: the desolate ruins of Jiaohe, a Han Dynasty
garrison town established to defend the borderlands.*

SERVES: 6

Sweet Bean Wontons

Wonton snacks, either sweet or savory, are a popular tea house treat. Made from prepared wonton wrappers and ready-made bean paste, these couldn't be more simple.

PREPARATION TIME: 30 minutes
COOKING TIME: 25 minutes

15 wonton wrappers	4 tbsps cold water
8oz sweet red bean paste	Oil for deep-frying
1 tbsp cornstarch	Honey

Take a wonton wrapper in the palm of your hand and place a little of the red bean paste slightly above the center.

Mix together the cornstarch and water and moisten the edge around the filling with a little of this paste. Fold the wrapper over, slightly off center, into a triangle shape. Pull the two bottom points together, using the cornstarch and water paste to stick them together. Turn inside out by gently pushing the filled center.

Heat enough oil in a wok for deep-fat frying and when hot, put in 4 of the filled wontons at a time. Cook until crisp and golden and remove to paper towels to drain. Repeat with the remaining filled wontons. Serve drizzled with honey.

Peking's Beihai Park, a popular haven for city dwellers.

MAKES: about 14
Chinese Bean Buns

Another recipe using bean paste, these little buns could be served equally well with tea or coffee or as a dessert.

PREPARATION TIME: about 2 hours, including proving time
COOKING TIME: about 30 minutes

¼ cup milk
⅓ cup fine granulated sugar
½ tsp salt
1½ tbsps shortening
¼ cup warm water
2 tsps dry yeast
1 egg, beaten
2¼ cups all-purpose flour

FILLING
⅓ cup sweet bean paste
2 tbsps fine granulated sugar
2 tbsps chopped walnuts
1 tbsp shortening

Bring the milk almost to the boil. Stir in the sugar, salt and shortening. Cool slightly. Put the warm water and yeast into a bowl and stir to mix. Add the lukewarm milk mixture. Add the beaten egg and 1 cup of the flour and beat until smooth. Add the remaining flour and mix to a dough. Turn dough out onto a well-floured board and knead until smooth and elastic. Place in a greased bowl. Brush the dough with oil and cover. Leave to rise in a warm place until doubled in size, about 1 hour.

Heat the filling ingredients together in a wok for 5-6 minutes until smooth and shiny. Remove and cool. Divide the filling into 12-14 portions. Knead the risen dough again for 2 minutes and then divide the dough into 12-14 portions. Flatten into thick, circular shapes 4 inches in diameter. Place a chopstick on each circle of dough to mark it in half, and then in half again. Cut along the marks to within ⅓ of the center. Place one portion of filling in the center of the dough circle and fold the cut ends in to meet in the center, to form a rosette. Secure by pinching ends of dough together. Place a piece of greased foil over the pinched ends and place the buns on a greased cookie tray. Brush with a little milk. Bake in a preheated 375°F oven for 20-25 minutes.

Facing page: water is an integral part of the appeal of Szechuan's Jiuzhaigou Nature Reserve, which also contains a conservation zone for pandas.

SERVES: 8

Eight Treasure Rice Pudding

This pudding is often served during the Chinese New Year celebrations. The Buddhists believe there are eight treasures in life and so the number has become absorbed into Chinese culture.

PREPARATION TIME: 15 minutes
COOKING TIME: 1¼ hours, in total

1¼ cups glutinous or sweet
   pudding rice
3 tbsps lard
2 tbsps sugar
15 dried red dates (jujubes), pitted
30 raisins
10 walnut halves
10 candied cherries
10 pieces of candied angelica,
   chopped

1 × ½lb can sweetened chestnut
   purée
or 1 cup sweetened red bean paste
Syrup
3 tbsps sugar
1¼ cups of cold water
1 tbsp cornstarch blended with
   2 tbsps water

Place the rice in a saucepan, cover with water and bring to the boil. Reduce heat, cover the pan tightly and cook the rice for 15 minutes or until the water is absorbed. Add 2 tbsps of the lard and the sugar to the cooked rice. Mix well. Brush a 3¾ cup capacity steaming mold with the remaining lard. Cover the bottom and sides with a thin layer of the rice mixture. Gently press a layer of the fruit and nuts into the rice. Cover with another layer of rice, much thicker this time. Fill the center with the chestnut purée or bean paste. Cover with the remaining rice. Press gently to flatten the top. Cover with a pleated circle of waxed paper. Secure with string.

   Steam the pudding for one hour. A few minutes before it is ready, make the syrup. Dissolve the sugar in the water, and bring to the boil. Stir in the cornstarch mixture and simmer gently until thickened. Invert the pudding onto a warmed serving platter, pour over the syrup and serve immediately.

Marble and wood in harmony in Grand View Garden, Peking.

Above left: the Yangtse River, unpredictable and potentially dangerous to navigate, flows through spectacular and menacing scenery. Above right: the great Zhujiang River Delta, an extremely fertile region around Kwangtung, which was the center of the Opium Wars in the nineteenth century.

MAKES: 30 cookies

Almond Cookies

In China these are often eaten as a between-meal snack. In Western style
cuisine, they make a good accompaniment to fruit or sorbet.

PREPARATION TIME: 10 minutes
COOKING TIME: 12-15 minutes per batch

---

1 stick butter or margarine	1 tsp baking powder
4 tbsps granulated sugar	Pinch salt
2 tbsps light brown sugar	¼ cup ground almonds, blanched
1 egg, beaten	or unblanched
Almond extract	2 tbsps water
1 cup all-purpose flour	30 whole blanched almonds

Cream the butter or margarine together with the two sugars until light and fluffy.
Divide the beaten egg in half and add half to the sugar mixture with a few drops of the
almond extract and beat until smooth. Reserve the remaining egg for later use. Sift the
flour, baking powder and salt into the egg mixture and add the ground almonds. Stir
well by hand. Shape the mixture into small balls and place well apart on a lightly
greased cookie sheet. Flatten slightly and press an almond on to the top of each
one.Mix the reserved egg with the water and brush each cookie before baking. Place in
a preheated 350°F oven and bake for 12-15 minutes. The cookies will be a pale golden
color when done.

*Facing page: the tomb of Wang Zhaojun near Hohhot, whose
site commemorates the marriage of a Chinese princess to the
King of Mongolia in the first century B.C.*

SERVES: 6-8

Almond Float with Fruit

Sweet dishes are not often served in the course of a Chinese meal.
Banquets are the exception, and this elegant fruit salad is
certainly special enough.

PREPARATION TIME: 25 minutes
SETTING TIME: 2 hours

---

1 envelope unflavored gelatin
6 tbsps cold water
⅓ cup sugar
1 cup milk
1 tsp almond extract
Few drops red or yellow food
    coloring (optional)

ALMOND SUGAR SYRUP
⅓ cup sugar
2 cups water
½ tsp almond extract

Fresh fruit such as kiwi, mango,
    pineapple, bananas, lychees,
    oranges or satsumas, peaches,
    berries, cherries, grapes or
    starfruit
Fresh mint for garnish

Allow the gelatin to soften in the cold water for about 10 minutes or until spongy. Put
in a large mixing bowl.

Bring ⅓ cup water to the boil and stir in the sugar. Pour into the gelatin and water
mixture and stir until the gelatin and sugar have dissolved. Add the milk, flavoring and
food coloring if using. Mix well and pour into an 8-inch-square pan. Chill in the
refrigerator until set.

Mix the sugar and water for the syrup together in a heavy-based pan. Cook over a
gentle heat until the sugar dissolves. Bring to the boil and allow to boil for about 2
minutes, or until the syrup thickens slightly. Add the almond extract and allow to cool
at room temperature. Chill in the refrigerator until ready to use.

Prepare the fruit and place in an attractive serving dish. Pour over the chilled syrup
and mix well. Cut the set almond float into 1-inch diamond shapes or cubes. Use a
spatula to remove them from the pan and stir them gently into the fruit mixture.
Decorate with sprigs of fresh mint to serve.

*Elaborate decorations adorn the roof of Xiqin Guild Hall in
Zigong, Szechuan province.*

SERVES: 4

Spun Fruits

Often called toffee fruits, this sweet consists of fruit fried in batter and coated with a thin, crisp caramel glaze.

PREPARATION TIME: 25 minutes
COOKING TIME: 10-15 minutes

BATTER
1 cup all-purpose flour, sifted
Pinch salt
1 egg
½ cup water and milk mixed half
    and half

1 large apple, peeled, cored and cut
    into 2-inch chunks

1 banana, peeled and cut into
    1-inch pieces
Oil for deep-frying
Ice water

CARAMEL SYRUP
1 cup sugar
3 tbsps water
1 tbsps oil

To prepare the batter, combine all the ingredients, except the oil for deep-frying, in a liquidizer or food processor and process to blend. Pour into a bowl and dip in the prepared fruit.

In a heavy-based saucepan, combine the sugar with the water and oil and cook over very low heat until the sugar dissolves. Bring to the boil and allow to cook rapidly until a pale caramel color.

While the sugar is dissolving, heat the oil in a wok and fry the batter-dipped fruit, a few pieces at a time. While the fruit is still hot and crisp, use chopsticks or a pair of tongs to dip the fruit into the hot caramel syrup. Stir each piece around to coat evenly. Dip immediately into ice water to harden the syrup and place each piece on a greased dish. Continue cooking all the fruit in the same way. Once the caramel has hardened and the fruit has cooled, transfer to a clean serving plate.

*A huge copper Buddha is the centerpiece of the Temple of the
Sleeping Beauty in the Western Hills of Peking.*

Top: a forty-four-foot-high Sakyamuni Buddha is one of many to be found at Yungang Grottoes in Shansi province. The carving of such a statue was considered to be a meritorious act - hence their large numbers. Above left: Sweet Dumplings. Above right: Stuffed Litchis.

MAKES: 10-12

Sweet Dumplings

The Chinese do not have a wide range of desserts and there are many variations on similar themes, using the same ingredients, of which red bean paste is one.

PREPARATION TIME: 10 minutes
COOKING TIME: 15-20 minutes

Salad or olive oil
½ cup fine granulated sugar
⅓ cup plain red bean paste
⅓ cup desiccated coconut

4 egg whites
1½ tbsps all-purpose flour
4 tbsps cornstarch
Confectioners' sugar

Heat 1 tbsp oil in a wok and add the sugar, bean paste and coconut. Stir-fry for 4-5 minutes until the sugar melts and the paste is smooth and shiny. Fry for a few minutes more and then allow to cool on a dish. Whip the egg whites until stiff and mix with the flour and cornstarch to a smooth batter. Beat well. Clean the wok and heat sufficient oil for deep-frying. Make 10-12 even-sized balls from the bean paste mixture. Dip each ball into the batter and then deep-fry for 3-4 minutes until golden and crisp. Fry a few at a time and drain on paper towels. Dust with sifted confectioners' sugar before serving.

SERVES: 6

Stuffed Litchis

This simple dessert makes the perfect end to a rich meal.

PREPARATION TIME: 20 minutes

3 cups canned litchis, stones removed
4-5 rings canned pineapple

Few drops vanilla extract or almond extract

Drain the litchis into a bowl, reserving the juice. Slice each pineapple ring into ½-inch-long strips. Press one or two strips of pineapple into each litchi. Arrange the pineapple-filled litchis in a deep serving dish. Mix the pineapple and litchi liquid with a few drops of almond extract. Spoon over the stuffed fruits. Serve well chilled. Alternatively, stuff the litchis with maraschino cherries, mango, canned pears, oranges, etc.

INDEX